T0049942

"This book is a heart opener. In some magical way, Kris is able to connect Mother Earth, creativity, entrepreneurship, and heart wisdom into one cohesive whole … I am certain that *Wildhearted Purpose* was divinely inspired, and that Kris has acted as a clear channel for Source in the writing of it."

—Coral Newberry,
Shamanic energy medicine practitioner
and spiritual teacher

"Kris has crafted vibrant guided journeys, soul-deep rituals, and words that read like poetry to show us how, through Mama Earth, we can remember ourselves and embrace our purpose."

—Samantha Brennan,
writer and editor

"If you've forgotten what kind of wildflower you are, this beautiful, poetic book can help you remember and rewild … Working slowly through the pages of this book might just be the life changing experience you are looking for."

—Andrea Mathews,
author of *Letting Go of Good*

"*Wildhearted Purpose* beautifully connects human nature to flowers that grow in all kinds of conditions … This book is a great resource, especially for those who are feeling self-conscious or out of place."

—Jessica Marie Baumgartner,
author of *The Magic of Nature*

"An uplifting and inspiring read that speaks directly to the soul … Weaving together story, breathtaking visualizations and journal practices, this book is not just an invitation, but a wildhearted embodiment of what it means to live deeply embedded in a Sacred New Earth."

—Heidi Wedd, herbalist, alchemist,
and author of *Wild Flower Walker*

"We all deserve to live happy, wild, and free; sometimes we just need to be reminded of the unbridled passionate people that we were always born to be. Through this book, Kris Franken will help guide you into your own wildhearted adventure within yourself."

—Emily A. Francis,
author of *The Taste of Joy*

WILDHEARTED
PURPOSE

ABOUT THE AUTHOR

Kris Franken is a spiritual author, intuitive, and wayshower. She guides other seekers home to the healing love and magnetic pull of their hearts. Kris is a visionary who sees the infinite potential for others through the wild wisdom of Mother Earth.

In addition to *Wildhearted Purpose*, Kris is also the author of *The Call of Intuition: How to Recognize & Honor Your Intuition, Instinct & Insight* and numerous sets of oracle cards, including *Soul Purpose, Spirit Animal,* and *Lightworker.*

Kris holds a bachelor's degree in psychology and sociology, is a certified Reiki healer and meditation teacher, and was a journalist for sixteen years. Originally from Toronto, Canada, Kris now gratefully calls Byron Bay on Bundjalung land, Australia, home.

WILDHEARTED PURPOSE

Embrace
Your Unique Calling
& the Unmapped
Path of Authenticity

LLEWELLYN PUBLICATIONS
Woodbury, Minnesota

FIRST EDITION

FIRST EDITION
First Printing, 2023

Book format by Mandie Brasington
Cover design by Cassie Willett
Interior line art illustrations by Llewellyn Art Department

Llewellyn Publications is a registered trademark of Llewellyn
    Worldwide Ltd.

Library of Congress Cataloging-in-Publication Data (Pending)
ISBN: 978-0-7387-7354-4

Llewellyn Worldwide Ltd. does not participate in, endorse, or have any authority or responsibility concerning private business transactions between our authors and the public.

All mail addressed to the author is forwarded but the publisher cannot, unless specifically instructed by the author, give out an address or phone number.

Any internet references contained in this work are current at publication time, but the publisher cannot guarantee that a specific location will continue to be maintained. Please refer to the publisher's website for links to authors' websites and other sources.

Llewellyn Publications
A Division of Llewellyn Worldwide Ltd.
2143 Wooddale Drive
Woodbury, MN 55125-2989
www.llewellyn.com

Printed in the United States of America

DEDICATED TO MAMA EARTH

You've been calling me home
Into your wild embrace
For so long

CONTENTS

Practices

Rituals

JOURNEYS

WILDFLOWERS BLOOM FREE

Wildflowers are breathtaking and rugged. They grow magnificently free, abundant and undisciplined by nature, completely in flow with the current of life, innocent and unruly, and at ease in their fully expanded state. Many wildflowers flourish in melancholy, undernourished soil, reminding us of our power for thriving, no matter our current situation or the experiences of our past.

When it comes to living your greatest purpose, let wildflowers be your muse.

Tamed flowers also bloom beautifully and radiate their own unique color and bliss, they just do it in an allocated position, placed in the ground by a flower director of sorts, watered and nourished regularly. But rarely do they offer the kind of weathered opulence or sweeping resplendence that undeterred blossoms provide.

As each wildflower nears the end of their short and sweet life, their seeds detach, scattering the next generation into the arms of the wind, flying high and wide to broaden their chances of continuing their uniquely beautiful lineage. Somehow, moved by the ancient wisdom of the elements, they end up where they belong, trusting implicitly in the perfectly designed dance of the Universe.

Like flowers, humans are born with a particular Soul imprint—each arriving from the seeds of their ancestors, long destined to walk this earth. And though we look and sound remarkably like those who created our physical form, we carry codes of light within us that are uniquely ours to discover and share.

As a child, you may have felt wild, as one with the sunshine, mud, rainbows, and jasmine, or you may have been boxed into a sculpted garden, kept neat, orderly, and disciplined. If you're anything like me, you may have tasted both kinds of childhoods.

Growing up between borders usually means there's healing to be sought for the bruises gained where we bumped up against the edges of life, as well as harnesses to be undone so that we may be the kind of sovereign adult who is able to live and love freely.

If you grew up and remained in flow with the ways of nature, then chances are you're still connected to your wild heart. This doesn't mean life is perfect, but it's likely that even now you live in tune with the wilderness.

Whatever your childhood looked like, it's through the process of unlearning inauthentic behaviors and healing outdated beliefs that you remember how to trust the true and natural wisdom within. It's through loving self-exploration that you find and devote yourself to your unique spark, releasing it from external restrictions and surrendering to all you came here to be. *This is radical authenticity.* To follow your inner pulse wherever the seasons take you is the wildhearted way.

Wildflowers have learned the importance of trusting their miraculous, ancient blueprint and aligning with the ultimate flow of life. They know that the most serendipitous and flourishing existence comes from yielding to the consciousness of light within each seed, all in divine timing.

To bloom along the overgrown and unmapped trails of life is why you're here.

THE REWILDING OF ME

At my desk where this book was crafted, I look out onto thousands of trees, a few rocky cliffs along a volcanic mountain range, a luscious waterfall, and a soft sunshower. I can hear one of the meandering creeks that flows through our property, pigeons flocking from tree to tree, and the sound of an eight-foot-long python getting cozy in my roof. I can feel new muscles forming in my legs from walking these hills and a sense of peace I've never fathomed before. I can smell the fresh flowers blooming on a tree planted long ago. I can taste a wild raspberry from an untamed vine and mint from one of its many generous sources.

I am in love with *the rewilding of me.*

All along my path I've respected the wild ones. I never truly fit in and didn't want to be like anyone else. I was happy to heed the weaving of the most raucous calling, like unpruned, rambunctious roses left to flourish in their own way. Sweet and thorny, lovingly protective, radiant and untethered. Replenishing themselves under the sun by day, soothing with the stars by night. Never given a curfew, instructions, or boundaries; that was my style.

I knew from an early age that I wasn't here to follow any other person, faith, system, or method. I'm here to discover the unique expression of the eternal spirit within me, and to gently guide others to do the same. I've come to know my Soul as the wisest guru and mentor I'll ever have in this and any other lifetime.

I grew up in churches where I was soothed by a familiar connection to the Masters and Priestesses I've known in past incarnations, supported by a community of kindhearted humans, and yet disillusioned by what was preached. It wasn't until I left the Church at the age of nineteen that I became curious about my spiritual truth. Soon enough I started unraveling a broader, more expansive and inclusive way of understanding life.

After wandering through the wilderness of study and work for many years toward an unknown destination, I eventually discovered and honored the most fundamental need in my career ... *to write*. In that moment, the axis on which I'd been traveling shifted, and I finally faced my true north.

I remember the axis shifting. I can still feel the quickening of my spirit, the way life began to radiate in a hundred more colors than usual—brighter, too. I can recall the energy that surged within me each day as I swept away everything else and focused on my own holy grail. Rejection didn't matter; other people's opinions became fairly obsolete. I only wanted to be nurtured, guided, and paid to be a writer. I didn't know the exact destination, and I felt lost and found all at the same time, but I was finally connected to the purpose of my heart.

Writing runs deep in the blueprint of my Soul; when I write, I dive into the cool and luscious waters of life, flowing with gifts and talents, satisfaction and service, passion and devotion. Writing *gives* me energy, revives my spirit, and calls me home.

After completing my first book *The Call of Intuition*, I discovered a new stream of purpose as a wayshower and mentor to help those who are wanting to rewild their lives toward the overgrown direction of their heart.

The rewilding of me is a mirror for the rewilding of others.

That's where the seed for this book was planted. In my devotion to ushering other curious seekers back into alignment with their heart, curated by their own divine purpose, illuminated by their own light, I unexpectedly and gratefully discovered this book was waiting to be written.

I've spent many hours connecting with teachers, healers, guides, and mentors so that I may know and live *my* purpose to its fullest. With every spark of interest, every word of advice, every exciting idea, I've consistently checked within my heart to see if it resonates. That's not to say my journey has been perfect; it's been painfully off-center at times. But each time I wander away from my knowing, I gently come home again.

You'll get to know more of my story throughout the pages ahead. You'll soon discover I'm the kind of woman who designs my own maps (and burns them at will), requires no permission slips, and likes to keep things organic, heartfelt, and serendipitous.

Adventuring with This Book

This book was cocreated with Mama Nature; it's a living guide whose intention is to show you the longing, direction, and wisdom of your abundantly wild and ferociously wise heart. This book isn't about guiding you onto some kind of predetermined process or successful framework that works for me. This book is not a prescription for purpose—rather, it wants to remind you of the astonishing purpose already imbued in the light of your being.

In the first part, you'll seed a *vision*; you'll discover and honor the dreams of your Soul that speak to your highest purpose and plant them into the ground of your existence. This visioning section is an important first step because when you pull back from life just a little, you're able to glimpse the purpose within your Soul. You're able to imagine your seemingly impossible dreams in full color. As you connect to your dreams, you'll feel them in your senses, you'll know them in your heart, and you'll allow your Soul to call them into your life in full bloom.

Visioning your purpose involves exploring your expansive inner landscape, healing all that beckons you off course, connecting deeply with your gifts, talents, and Soul medicine, and trusting in the rugged process of dreaming your purpose into life.

In the second part, you'll have the opportunity to take your vision and *grow* a unique design from your visionary seeds. The designing process takes your dreamy ideas and puts them down onto paper. It's the seed sprouting from the soil—visible, real, and promising. It brings form to your imagination and structure to your desires.

You'll be inspired to release all maps that don't belong to you, find the truth that radiates through all that you are, get comfortable with risk, and courageously design a purpose that feels completely authentic.

In the third and final part, you'll be inspired to *bloom* as your purpose every day from the buds of your fertile heart. You'll connect directly to the light within you, your inimitable essence, and explore rituals and practices that will infuse your purpose in your existence day by day.

Living your purpose is a cyclical process that works in harmony with your community and with nature. It's about showing up in your joyfully purposeful presence and living in service to others while honoring your own heart.

I've always believed in nature as the greatest teacher of them all, so I called on Mama Nature to create this book with me. (Or perhaps She had the idea first and reeled me into this; I'm not sure.) She told me stories of the earth and the cosmos that became the inspiration for each idea, chapter, and section. She's been with me the whole way, and I hope you enjoy the many adventures She wants to take you on throughout these pages.

As you flow through this book, you'll be taken on wildhearted meditative "Journeys" into nature to learn directly from Her. These journeys may feel like fun, imaginative adventures, or they may touch you deeply and help you process dense emotions and old pain. Go gently and allow yourself to feel all that comes up for you. Pause as much as you need to allow these journeys to integrate into your life. Allow these passages to enliven an inner wilderness where you can learn, create, and grow.

You'll also discover "Soul Prompts" to inspire a conscious understanding of your life through the power of the written word. Keep a journal close as you read this book so you can jot down your dreams, desires, and downloads in one place.

I've also shared many sacred "Rituals" to help embody your purpose through regular everyday activities. Take what resonates from these and use them to deepen your daily spiritual practice. Your heart will show you what it's craving more of.

This book aims to be all the loving motivation you need to *adventure* into the light within you and connect to the greatest purpose of all … *yours*.

Are you ready to remember and reclaim your own wildhearted purpose? Let's begin.

Part One
SEED A VISION

At the beginning of every purposeful project, heartfelt creation, ambitious collaboration, or career move is the spark, the bright idea that sets it all into sweet, synchronistic motion.

Within the spark, the golden seed, the initial whisper of promise, lives all the information and energy needed for the entire process. This information is a blueprint, a divine design that holds a micro plan for the macro life, just as the flower seed holds the vision and wisdom for the plant that will grow from it.

Your Soul is a perfect fragment of Source. Your purpose lives within the blueprint of your Soul, which, like a sunflower in full bloom, contains many seeds of golden light. Anything purposeful, creative, imaginative, truthful, aligned, and unique you do begins with a spark from your Soul's own light.

Some people plant seeds all the time but don't water them, some are hesitant to plant any seeds at all, while others throw seeds into the air, hoping they'll fortuitously land and bloom. Intentionally planting seeds and taking care of them means your dreams will grow into abundant blessings; this is done by working initially on a vision, which comes straight from your blueprint.

The first part of this book is all about the vision. Dreaming this dream may take a few days or much longer; it may come easily or feel like a bountiful stretch of all your capabilities. Your dreams matter.

Without these dreams and visions, you won't have the anchor points to come back to along the intuitive journey of your wild purpose. And while it's often necessary for the vision to change and flow along the way, your preparedness will hold you to the original intention, the multidimensional design that arose from the radiance of your Soul.

Here's how you create that luminous vision.

Chapter 1

IMAGINE YOUR
WILDEST PURPOSE

"Listen to the world around you. Open your heart.
Rebalance. And enjoy your journey."[1]
—ARIN MURPHY-HISCOCK

This first chapter is about the initial brave moment you decide to live the courageous life designed by your Soul. When this happens, you may find yourself suddenly navigating a rugged, fresh route. From utterly predictable to naturally impulsive. From crowded and rowdy to expansive and serene. One minute you're matching each step to the footprints in front of you, the next you're walking at your own pace, creating your own gentle path.

There may not be an obvious warning you're veering off course; the signs could be subtle. You can look all around you for directions into nature, but inevitably it's an inner pull, an inescapable desire to leave the pavement for the tall grass, to walk away from the obvious into the open air.

1. Arin Murphy-Hiscock, *The Green Witch: Your Complete Guide to the Natural Magic of Herbs, Flowers, Essential Oils, and More* (Avon, MA: Adams Media, 2017), 10.

Yours Is the Wildest Path

This is how the wild calls you: in an impulsive moment of joy, in a timeless connection to awe, in a rebellious act of nonconformity, or in a simple, open-hearted choice. When you say yes to the wild, you're saying yes to the ancient agency of love within you.

· Journey ·
Into the Infinite Unknown

Imagine how it would feel to be called by the wild. There you are, walking on a paved asphalt path—black, hot, and unforgiving. Your feet ache. You can't see the scenery for all those walking in front of, behind, and beside you. Your eyes are sore. You're thirsty for something, and water won't satiate the craving. The crowd is so ceaselessly noisy that you haven't heard the whispers of your heart for a long time.

Taking your shoes off and tucking them into your bag, you spontaneously step off the paved track. The dirt is soft, soothing your stifled feet; soon there are rocks to massage away your tension, then grass to amuse your bare soles. At first you wobble, so used to the flat predictability of the pavement and the shackles of your shoes. Before long, your feet and legs come alive, singing with their newfound connection to the earth.

You're not sure where you're headed, but somehow you know you're facing the right direction. You're excited and curious about *all* of life. A dam has burst within the chambers of your heart, and you're breathlessly following the rapture that ensues.

After a few hours of wandering according to the bliss of your being, it rains. Without shelter, you feel momentarily vulnerable, having been disconnected from your inner nature for so long. Looking around, you see only fields of flowers and shrubs—nothing to duck under for a spell. The rain falls harder, insisting on sur-render. With a deep breath, you drop your bag, take off your hat, relax your shoulders, and open to the storm.

When the thunder rolls toward you, you breathe in the crisp, cleansing air of the tempest. As the lightning strikes in the distance, you sing for joy. After a while, fearful, lonely thoughts come to the surface. Enduring a storm outside without an umbrella, coat, or shelter is too much to bear for an overwhelming moment. You listen, accept, and honor each emotion before letting it go, surrendering it into the healing waters. When all has been heard and healed, you feel safe and steady.

You look around and see no one to share this moment with, the path long gone from your senses. You wish for a friend to dance with in the rain; your prayer is answered as a flock of strik-ing white birds fly out of the darkest cloud, their screech a wel-come note in the symphony of the storm. They swoop down to you, opening their wings at full measure, looking right at you. You squeal with them, delighted at their powerful presence.

As they fly away, the wind eases, the rain slows, and the sun pierces through the clouds, causing a rainbow to tint the sky. This precious rainbow, unable to be bought or grasped, folded up or traded, is a welcome sign from nature, and indeed from the most divine nature within you, that this venturous move to embark on an unknown journey will be blessed until the end.

With soaking wet clothes and a smile so big it hurts, you collect your gear and move onward under a blanket of the sun's humid rays.

THE WILDEST VERSION OF YOU

When you're living your true purpose, the path you walk on isn't paved or smooth—it's overgrown and underground, untrod-den and disruptive, messy and tangled in places. It's a disarray of vines and flowers, shrubs and sand, logs and dirt, weeds and trees, woven with nature's own vibrant lifeforce, tended to by bees and butterflies, guarded by spiders and snakes, lit by stars and sunshine, watered by healing rain, and seen to by divine magic. It's an unmapped, endless route over parched desert and exhilarating mountains, under cleansing waterfalls and humbling storms, through peaceful gullies and raucous fields of wildflowers.

Gazing ahead, there's no way of telling what lies before you or where to go. The songlines you must walk if you desire to fulfill your dreams aren't drawn on the ground or mapped on a piece of paper, they're tucked inside the epicenter of your heart.

You'll find the clearest vision of your purpose when you close your eyes, open your heart, and look within; when you learn to conceive each part of your course according to the magnetic pull of your inner core, when you grow so quiet you can hear the ancient stars awakening within your light. You'll find it when you learn to surrender anything and everything that isn't yours to carry, and when you trust completely in the highest plan for your life.

In the wilderness there is no map, no logical plan, no predetermined timelines, no pathway of perfect advice to get you to the next vista, and no faultless earthly guide to follow. It's *all* within you ... *the wildest version of you.*

Devotion to your wise heart doesn't mean you'll be on your own the whole distance. You're lovingly guided by Mother Gaia, who called you here for an important reason. She loves you and will take care of you as you surrender into Her; She is the reason you are awakening to your purpose on a more expansive level. Walking beside you are Nature and Animal Spirits, who have endless wisdom, healing, and play to share; plus there are many other beings of light who celebrate you as you navigate life aligned with the orbit of your heart.

You'll also meet many other humans throughout this adventure. Our routes are destined to meet with one another, for support and comfort, for love and intimacy, for inspiration and celebration, and for lessons and resilience. The thoughts and beliefs of your own being will create a unique vibration each day that will draw people close to your path. Some will stay a long while, others only for a moment. Your community will always come when you need them.

The wildest version of you is calling to you now. To shine in your full radiance and truth each day. To live the life your Soul imagines. To share the gifts and talents that are a vital part of your being. To claim the abundance that is already yours. And to walk each step barefoot in faith that you're heading in the direction of your heart.

· RITUAL ·
Barefoot Adventure in Nature

Take yourself on an adventure. Find a beautiful, safe place in nature that allows you to walk without a map or on a path. You can do this on a beach, a grassy field, or in among the trees; the point is to create an adventure that feels comfortable and fun, while also unknown and wild.

Take your time. Revel in bare feet if that's easy for you. Walk mindfully without taking any photos or looking at your phone. Tune in to your body and how it feels; ask it where it wants to go. Listen to the messages and stories of Gaia. Sit on a rock and feel the slow vibration. Place your hand on a tree and allow the healing to move through you. Open your heart to the birdsong and any other sounds from animals. Feel the wind, sun, earth, and water as a part of you. Let this connection reset your inner compass, refresh the vision of your purpose, and reinstate your intention for being alive and awake to your heart. As you leave, give thanks for your experience.

When you return home, draw your experience in your journal without using words. Allow yourself to be fully expressive and creative with color and texture. Honor yourself for your adventure and commit to regular time in the wilderness.

When your drawing is complete, look at the symbolism of all the natural elements and how they relate to the unfolding vision of your purpose. What does each aspect of the drawing represent? It could be a one-word answer or an in-depth consideration. Acknowledge your drawing and allow it to inspire the visions of your life, work, and play.

Immeasurable Trust in the Overgrowth

Living from the heart isn't always easy. Often, we encounter obstacles that seem overwhelming. Yet, when they are seen with love, they may simply be representing our inner state. With compassion for ourselves, clarity comes and shines a light whenever we need it so we can make it through the overgrowth with easeful surrender.

· Journey ·
As Within, So Without

In the next vision of this adventure, see yourself quietly walking your unique passage through nature for days, delighting in the earth's abundance as you lovingly rewild the lifeforce within. After much peace, you encounter twisted, thorny, bristly, unkempt vines and branches before you. The kind that can't easily be climbed over or walked around.

Your feet long to move forward, to keep up with the momentum you've created, but you're stuck, heavy with the nature of the task ahead. You're new to this kind of work, and without the appropriate tools, you fumble to make a start. It takes you all morning to pull at the branches and tear down the vines, and still you aren't able to progress. Hands bleeding, you pause to clean them, bandage them, and take a rest for lunch.

Sitting against a tree, you notice a lizard approach the thick forest. Effortlessly the lizard scuttles over each branch like a bridge, moving quickly to his destination and discovering fresh insects to munch along the way. Soon a snake appears and, without pausing, it slips between each fallen branch, stealing along the underside and grateful for the shade.

You realize that each creature approaches the scrub with ease and uses the overgrowth to its advantage. You close your eyes and ask your heart, "How do I find a way through without damaging nature or hurting my body?" Your heart replies, "The branches are possibilities, inner thoughts; leave them for now. The vines are your old beliefs, suffocating your thoughts and blocking them from the light. Go to the root of each vine to know where they came from. With easeful surrender and *inner* strength, you will know how to set them free and make it through."

You follow a vine to its root; it's thin and dry and looks easy to wrench from the ground. You pull as hard as you can, but it doesn't budge. You pull harder and your hand slips, causing thorns to break off into your skin.

Once you've taken time to clean your hand, you go back to the vine with a softer energy. Remembering the words of your own wise heart, you tune in to the vine. It feels like a tangle of frustration. You welcome this and send a prayer of release to its core; then, when you feel a shift, you gently pull it free. In seconds, the whole vine unwraps itself from other vines and branches and lands out of the way at the side of the overgrowth. With a

renewed sense of confidence and unexpected delight, you find the
next vine. It's much thicker and thornier. Holding it, you feel dense
with repressed anger. You send the root love all the way down,
knowing that you created it in fear and only love can set it free.
The anger loosens, melts, transforms. As you gently tug on it, it
dissolves, and you pull it out. After a short while of clearing all the
roots from the earth and healing the emotions from your heart,
you look up. All the vines are clear; the sun is sprinkling through
the leaves, and a path under branches, framed by thick tree roots,
lies ahead. With a grateful breath, you walk with an easy spirit and
an earthly ecstasy through the glowing forest.

SURRENDERING TO YOUR
UNRULY NATURE

Trusting in your intuitive, spontaneous, illogical heart requires
immeasurable trust in the unknown. Looking ahead on your wild
path, you won't find anyone showing you the way because no
one else could possibly have your way figured out. You can't follow anyone else's path because your steps will feel misaligned and
untrue.

As you follow the direction of your Soul's inner knowing,
expect a lot of thick overgrowth at times. Welcome and embrace
it. Disorderly vines as dense emotions and strong branches as
recurrent thoughts are all healing and growing opportunities.
Unraveling and surrendering your emotions will make room for
clearer thoughts, which will create more expansive and fruitful
possibilities in your life.

In nature, you'll find more than vines to clear; there are all
kinds of hurdles, real and symbolic, to embrace. Removing obstacles from your path will build muscles of resilience in your being.
Rolling logs can be turned into boundaries, weeding can provide

medicinal benefits, pruning shrubs sheds stale energy, and cutting long grass will open you up to an expansive view of the place you've set out to explore.

Dissolving thorny vines by their roots will mean fewer snags from old beliefs along the way of discovering and expressing your greatness. The overgrowth of vines essentially represents the challenges created in the past. Fear, despair, anxiety, disillusionment, frustration, trauma, and anger will show up when they're ready to be seen and healed. Nature creates the optimal tension for us to witness and surrender these heavy emotions; there's no need to go chasing after them. When they show up, if they're repressed, denied, or ignored, they can create difficulties on your journey.

The only way is to *surrender to your unruly nature.*

Caroline Myss succinctly expresses the weight of outdated beliefs. I met with Caroline in Brisbane in early 2020. With her, I felt such powerful presence; she has a devotion to her intuition and a conviction to her message, which I anticipated from reading many of her books, but I was still delighted at how empowered I felt to meet her in person.

In *Anatomy of the Spirit*, she writes, "Becoming conscious requires stamina. It is extremely challenging, and often very painful, to evaluate our own personal beliefs and separate ourselves from those that no longer support our growth. Change is the nature of life, and external and internal change is constant. When we change inwardly, we outgrow certain belief patterns and strengthen others."[2]

Healing, change, and growth are necessarily interwoven into all wildcrafted adventures; it's how we become our most expansive, abundant, and conscious self. It's when we tend to the emotional

2.   Caroline Myss, *Anatomy of the Spirit: The Seven Stages of Power and Healing* (Great Britain: Bantam Books, 1997), 110–111.

vines with full responsibility and unconditional love that we're able to see, feel, and swing on the branches of possibility. This is where a purposeful vision gains clarity and beauty, depth and integrity, ease and freedom. Healing layer after layer of weighty emotions and misaligned beliefs helps you become more connected to the limitless present.

When the overgrowth becomes too much and you feel confused, overwhelmed, lost, or disconnected, know that you're exactly where you're meant to be, and the way onward can be found in sacred stillness. Cease fighting your blocks and inhibitions and pause to come home to your Soul. Find a quiet place to relax and close your eyes. Breathe in and out. Calm your mind. Let all the swirling, hazy emotions melt away into the loving earth beneath you. Feel all that needs to move through you. Cry a river of tears, stomp your feet on the ground, sigh loudly, or move your limbs. When you're done, let it all go. Anchor your heart into the heart of Gaia. Give thanks, breathe in pure lifeforce, and open your eyes.

You may be surprised at what's in front of you. The shrubs of confusion may have receded; heavy clouds of unease, cleared; and vines blocking your spacious vision, melted away into the forest. Sacred stillness, unwavering acceptance, and gentle *surrender to your unruly nature* are the best tools to cleanse your field and your vision.

Look around your life at how everything is laid out before you—all the flowers and thorns, vines and branches, clouds and rainbows, and everything between. See it all as perfect. All of it. You have created this, and you have the opportunity every day to create something different if you wish. Know that there is no right or wrong, good or bad, better or worse. It all just *is*, and if it's anything other than perfect in your mind, your body and energy will resist it and angst over what needs to be fixed. Your vision for your future is created with ease when you can look around in this moment and see abundance with gratitude.

The overgrowth is a gift from life itself. The divine garden of life is reflecting all you carry within your being. You, the responsible, empowered gardener, have many opportunities each day to tend to your dreams and purpose with love and a vision for the highest good.

Don't be afraid to turn over the dirt and start again.

When it comes to living your purpose, start with a foundation of good health, the solid ground on which you walk, dance, sleep, and create. The overall state of your physical, mental, and spiritual health affects everything you do. Heal what you can when difficulties come into your awareness. Before you go to bed each night, thank your body for healing itself deeply as you sleep. Call in healers of the highest integrity and holistic understanding to work with you. As you heal, you enrich the soil from which all your life blooms. Without healing, your vision is obscured, clouded, darkened by that which lingers.

If you're devoted to healing, you'll organically awaken to the beliefs seeded in your being, anointing them with your consciousness, surrendering all that doesn't support your most bountiful growth.

Whenever I feel as though I'm blocked from accessing financial abundance, meaningful connections, radiant joy, or creative flow, I go deep into the wilderness within to discover what old beliefs, fears, densities, challenges, or traumas are in the way. If I can't recalibrate this flow of energy myself, I'll connect with a healer who can show me the way.

One of the signs I know there's a block is not only the lack of what I desire in my life, but also the language I use about that particular aspect. Words—thought or vocalized—such as *I'm struggling with money, I wish I had more clients, life is so stressful,* or *business is slow and draining* can offer insights into the kind of overgrowth tripping you on your path. All limiting beliefs come from old emotions that often stem from confrontation or conflict. Feeling the emotions of each heavy belief and surrendering them to love will open a path of possibility where you can visualize and create all you desire.

Life is abundant. Love the process of your life. You incarnated to call in a New Earth; this isn't a straightforward or simple process. Yours is no ordinary life. There is much to be cleared—past lives, karma, childhood, trauma—so that you may be at ease within yourself and at peace no matter what. Peace is a powerful place for transcending the everyday and accessing the wildest vision of your purpose.

Allow life to show you what's next for your holistic healing, spiritual activation, and evolution of purpose.

Surrender to your unruly nature and watch the miracles grow all around you.

· PRACTICE ·
Conscious Manifesto Soul Prompts

When you become conscious of the regular self-talk you use, you'll be able to sense the negative beliefs when they appear in your mind. Some are remarkably sneaky; others will stand out. When you notice them, hold them gently and let the following process unfold.

- In your journal, capture these beliefs by writing them down, whether you feel they're true or not.

- What words stand out or feel heaviest? Circle them and consider the emotion behind them. Write down the dense emotions you feel may have created this thought. If *money* stands out, look at what is so edgy about money. Does money feel scarce, overly important, shameful, or unsafe? Note this and ask your heart what else you need to know.

- Take a look back through your life to see where the cause of this particular emotional attachment to the thought came from. Even if it takes a while, stay with this until you get to the root cause. You may hear a story, see a memory or symbol, or resonate with a knowing from a past life. Write down whatever comes to you. Forgive whoever needs forgiveness, including yourself. You'll feel a sense of relief in your being when you get to the root, even if it's not completely conscious. Linger in this state for a moment and let the emotion go. It may sound simple, but this is miraculously powerful work.

- Imagine there's a violet flame wrapped around your page of thoughts and emotions. This alchemical flame transforms energy from one state to another because energy cannot be created or destroyed, only transmuted or transformed. Allow the cool, violet flames to transform these emotions into higher ways of being. When you feel a shift, write down what the old emotion has become. Shame may become empowerment, guilt may become generosity, or anger may become wisdom.

- In alignment with these new emotions, create manifestos to inspire fresh beliefs for your life. Write these in the first person (I, me, or my) and keep them positive and in the present tense, such as "I am empowered to give and receive money mindfully and with ease." Take the ones that feel the most powerful and write them down where you'll see them regularly. You may wish to write them in color and add drawings, sacred geometry, or creative lettering. This will sharpen your vision for your deeper purpose to come into being.

- Revel in the space you've created and the light that pours in after this process.

WEAVE TOGETHER DREAMS AND DESTINY

Your Ancestors cleared the way for you over eons of time, weaving together their magic, love, and creation, healing themselves, tending to the earth, all for future generations. Many of those who have passed on to higher realms are gently watching over you and loving your every courageous move. Their energy cannot die; it remains on the earth plane for you to access and learn from with respect and gratitude. You are the miracle they've been praying for.

· JOURNEY ·
You Belong to the Ancient Ones

Picture yourself asleep one long winter's night when your Ancestors visit you in a dream more real and vivid than most. In this dream, you lie still in a cave as they paint your body with colors of the earth and stars. You sit in rapture as they dance around you, playing instruments and singing in their ancient, native language. You listen as they tell you stories of Eagle and Jaguar, Snake and Bear, waterways and mountains, trees and earth medicine.

The vision you remember the clearest is when they take you outside to a creek and sit across from you, holding fresh sweetgrass in their hands. Together, you divide the grass into three sections, weaving each together until a strong braid is made. Twelve elders sit in a circle around you, each taking turns holding the grass with you, whispering into the grass as it's woven, speaking of the images they see in your Soul. Some recognize you as a star being, others as a warrior. Some see you as your Spirit Animal, some as the rainbow radiance of your aura. One by one, they infuse the fragrant grass with visions of your spirit.

On waking, you vow to honor your Ancestors and their endless love for you. You feel them with you in your tent, smiling at your reverence.

THE DREAMS OF YOUR HEART

Night dreams of symbols and journeys, whispers and memories, all have an impact on your life, whether you remember them or not. They are journeys of the Soul that are healing what has been and weaving magic in preparation for what is to come. Some of the greatest shifts in our lives happen without our conscious awareness or participation.

Daydreams of creating, coloring, writing, designing, playing, orchestrating, performing, dancing, healing, and loving are of cosmic importance. While egoic dreams of being globally famous or ridiculously wealthy stem from some form of insecurity, *the dreams of your heart* command respect and space to come to life.

Dreams, confirmation, inspiration, revelations, and visions can come in the most unexpected moments. Sometimes dreams come in subtle messages that point to the desires of our heart and the destiny in our Soul. They are so easy to sweep away from consciousness, their importance lost, their potency, drowned in the noise of life. Without acknowledgment, they can seemingly vanish, hiding under the well-trodden rug of busy-ness.

Life gives us plenty of opportunities to follow the passageway of our dreams. Our destiny doesn't stop pulling at us, calling us into the realm of our ultimate possibilities. Sometimes the pull feels like a joyful connection to what feels blissful and true; other times, it's a push away from what's uncomfortable. We can never truly be comfortable in a job, career, house, relationship, or place that doesn't align with our innermost essence.

On the days you notice the niggling discomfort of misalignment, don't ignore, suppress, distract, or run from it. All it's asking is to be acknowledged. Feel into it fully and expand your being to accommodate this aspect that feels out of sync. When you're ready, and without waiting too long, ask what it wants to show you.

You might think you don't want to hear the answer; that's simply not true. It's your ego who doesn't want to hear the answer. It's your constrictive, fearful, limited ego who doesn't want to change, expand, or grow. It's your outdated beliefs that keep you trapped in smallness, afraid of your wider community, of being wholly seen and wildly successful.

Your ego, your past, and your wounds aren't you. You are a luminous light of infinite possibilities. And the infinite you *wants* all those answers, golden or gritty, easy or challenging. It wants to peer into the shadow and learn from anything that hurts or feels unwanted, to fertilize the dark soil with wisdom and grow higher where the light shines. Your discomfort is not a mistake, it's a sign from your Soul that you've strayed away from inner harmony.

The dreams of your heart are the visions that call your destiny to you.

When the particles and fragments of your ecstatic dreams flow toward you, notice them. Bring them close. Nurture them until they piece themselves together within the fabric of your heart. They may be sweet and subtle or resounding and righteous; they may seem logical or subliminal; they may feel exciting or daunting. Move with them as they take shape.

Dreams may make themselves known in the adventure of sleep or they may come to you in visions, daydreams, conversations, and opportunities. You may have experiences in nature that remind you of your true self and the dreams that are waiting to be noticed. Dreams are not born from competition or jealousy, desperation or possessiveness, attachments or insecurity—only from love. You'll know which dreams are meant for you by the way they feel: expansive, joyful, liberating, and fulfilling.

As you weave these dreams from the ethers into your life with the assistance of the Elders and Ancestors of your lineage and the land you live on, they braid together like sweetgrass, thick and strong, blessed and inspired, sacred and earthly.

A strong purpose is woven with complementary aspects. Life wants you to explore the many gifts and talents of your ancient being, to be devoted but not fastidious, prismatic but not scattered. You are being called to be all you are—no less, not simplified to one isolated part of your purpose, but an evolving and multifaceted being of light, truth, love, and service.

It all takes time to weave together, and there will be many moments you'll need to reweave certain aspects of your life, your career, and your place in your community. There's no denying the moments of chaos and tragedy that bring life undone. It's these times when you are able to pause and honor what needs to be surrendered, to gather the loose grass and rebraid your purpose, steeping the healing process.

Writing is only one thread of the whole braid of my purpose. It's a strong and important one; it gives me so much pleasure and joy, but it was never meant to be my *everything*.

I began having unexpected daydreams about Reiki healing around my fortieth birthday. I had never considered using my hands to channel energy healing for others, but while receiving this beautiful healing from others, my heart consistently nudged me toward learning this ancient healing art. Receiving my Reiki I and II certificates felt like being handed a key that opened a whole new way of being in my life; insightful psychic access became easier, and I began to see all around me in multidimensional layers of reality. I now share healing and activating energy with others in ways that go beyond Reiki, mostly through sound and meditative journeys, but I can see clearly through loving hindsight how important it was for me to take that step.

A few years after becoming a certified Reiki healer, my braid of purpose became thicker when I took up mentoring. It felt like a natural extension of who I was, and yet it was also a surprising new pathway. As I began working with clients who wanted clarity on their Soul's path, my own journey became awash with opportunities. I've now worked with many people all over the world, and each session brings me a sense of sublime service. All through my life, I have received visions for friends when they spoke of feeling lost on their career path. These visions have always felt easy and natural, and now that I'm sharing them with clients, they're helping more people reclaim *the dreams of their hearts*.

I have a braid of dried sweetgrass I bought from a Northern American Indigenous man shortly after I discovered my Canadian Cree Indigenous lineage through my Mom's family. This also happened around the time I turned forty—a powerful year. The braid sits on my altar, reminding me of the ancestral power within me and my children as I serve as a wayshower for others.

There will be whispers and nudges, signs and clues all along your journey, like sweetgrass growing along a wild swamp. Gather them up in your arms like treasures. Keep them close, weave them lovingly, follow their counsel, and allow them to strengthen your lifelong purpose. The more you weave, the stronger and more resilient your vision will be.

· PRACTICE ·
Dream Journal Soul Prompts

A dream journal isn't only inspiring and helpful for keeping in touch with your visions and journeys at night, but also for bringing your daydreams into reality through ink on paper. You may want to take a new journal and keep it just for dreams, or you can flip your journal and use the back section.

When you write an idea or wish down, you pull it from the higher dimensions into the earth plane. This feels more real to your mind than the whispers and figments of your dreams. Your mind will question it, naturally, wanting to know how and when it will happen. Allow the Universe to deliver the dream into your life whenever it's for your highest good, and live as though life is conspiring in your favor every day. Try these ideas to make your dreams come true.

- Each morning, write down all your night dreams as soon as you wake. Try not to move too much, look at screens, or talk to anyone before you do this so you remember as much as possible. Write down all the interesting, boring, and peculiar aspects of the dream without needing to make any sense of it. Come back to your night dreams every now and then as they may have more meaning in the future.

- Jot down all the whimsical daydreams your heart desires. Don't limit yourself in the slightest! At the end of the month or year, you can look back and see what makes you smile with pride and notice what came true. Messages such as "I want to live on an island and make jewelry from shells" or "Today a friend told me I tell the most engaging stories and she thought I should become a speaker or teacher" are a delight to remember and treasure. And you just never know where they may take you.

- There are endless whispers from the Universe that come to us in signs, symbols, nature, animals, songs, and all kinds of communication. We are all dreaming our life into reality with the Universe. Write down the messages you've noticed lately and what you feel they mean in your journal. The more you take notice, the more is revealed.

DEEPER MEANING IN THE UNDERGROWTH

Without meaning in our lives, our purpose, and our service, it's easy to feel empty, awash with uncertainties and insecurities. Blown about by tides of others' making, we don't get the chance to drop our anchor where we most desire. True meaning comes from within, and when we dig deep to find it and create a foundation with it, fulfillment and joy have a fertile place to bloom from.

· JOURNEY ·
Blessed to Be a Witness

As you envision the next part of your journey, you notice a pattern that appears in your exploring in the way you relate to nature.

For months now, you've been cutting off branches to make spears and fire, plucking flowers for offerings and personal healing, pulling up grass to make baskets and music, and eating nature's edible gifts you find growing plentifully.

Your heart overflows with gratitude and light, and yet you haven't given back to nature much beyond your offerings and thanks. Once this occurs to you, you set an intention to be with nature so intimately that you would generously add to its abundance and regeneration.

You've been camping in the same area for a while. Each day you come to know the trees as they change in the cooler weather, breathing with them, watching the leaves and seedpods dropping and dancing. You've been working with flowers, propagating their abundant beauty all over the land. You've been digging your hands into the earth, sensing the nutrients and energetically exchanging a symbiotic balance within the soil. You've been relocating vines, wrapping them where they're needed so they don't suffocate the trees. You've created a flourishing space for birds, bees, and butterflies to access all they need throughout the winter months.

The resulting, flourishing wild around you is coming to life within you.

While deepening your access to your intuition and ability to flow with the elements, over time you've noticed subtle changes in nature. The sound of birds is louder, the early winter sun is more accessible, the flowers bloom through once-deserted fields, and a native beehive is in the making halfway up the tallest tree.

Connecting with nature all around you is a blissful experience of satisfaction that has inspired a rewilding of your lifeforce. You feel vitally alive and connected. You feel at home in this luscious setting where you have purpose and meaning. You have a reason to stay, contribute, and thrive within this glorious expanse.

Soul sisters and brothers find you and linger awhile to cocreate paradise with you. Encouraged by your endeavors, they stay to learn and listen, teach and share. You soak up their wisdom, they revel in your realm. Some stay for a night, others for weeks. Without attachments or expectations, you delight in this fluid communion with nature and other seekers.

One day, you go foraging in an oversized bush full of juicy berries that grew after a recent pruning. As you revel in the sweet rewards, you notice a large spider at an underground entrance to its home in the tree trunk. When you look closer, unafraid and curious, the spider tries to move away from you, but is unable to. Two feet are caught in fresh sap from the tree. You smile at the spider, reassuring it that it's safe and you're here to help. A connection is made; you both feel relief and love. You reach for a small stick, dip it in some dew inside the petals of a large lilium plant, and gently rub the sap off the spider's legs.

After the spider returns to its home, you sit next to the tree to integrate your experience. You feel like a temporary custodian and student of this beautiful land. It isn't yours, and yet you've become an intrinsic part of it and all the beings who dwell here.

PURPOSE GROWS WHERE MEANING FLOWS

It's in our nature as humans to seek happiness and pleasure in our lives; when this is healthy and balanced, these inner states are clear indicators we're connected to our truth. But without meaning, we lose our balance and sense of purpose. As you initiate your vision, meaning will bring depth into the picture as pleasure brings elevation.

What is meaning? We're all on a search for it in some way; we feel unclear and unsteady without it. True meaning comes from within, not from an external source. It's our inherent meaning that comes to life through loving service. It's not the trees, flowers, spiders, or berries that give us meaning, it's our interaction with them, and the spark that illuminates within us in communion with what matters to us, that establishes a meaningful life.

Meaning is personal and an essential part of who you are.

When you follow the whims of your ego, searching *outwardly* for what gives you fleeting amusement, you may become so caught in a cycle of vast emptiness and desperate longing that you lose sight of the deeper connection to your own meaningful heart.

When you tune your vision in to what brings meaning alive *within* you, you're able to lift yourself out of cycles of unfulfillment and into a higher way of living, serving, connecting, loving, and truly enjoying life. It's in the deepening of your attention to life that you rise higher into purpose.

Meaning feels long-term and bone-deep. When you envision a task or creation that aligns with your values and then surrender the outcome to the highest good, you find your purpose.

Purpose grows where meaning flows.

Your personal values speak to the gifts of your Soul. Knowing your core values is essential when dreaming in your vision. It's in the process of letting go of doubts, connecting with your heart, and sharing your service with others that you weave a life rich with meaningful joy and heartfelt bliss.

When you're distracted, mindlessly busy, or trapped in obsessions of materialism and superficiality, it's difficult to gain enough clarity around the vision that draws you into your purpose. It's in the undergrowth, below the captivating sweetness of life, that claims your inimitable qualities that bring you into harmony with the earth and all who dwell on it.

At the deepest level, we're all seeking harmony with the one heart that connects us all. As we heal ourselves, serve each other, and tend to the earth, we feel the harmony that our heart has been yearning for all along. True satisfaction is found on the path of reverence, compassion, and peace, not on the ego's path of swift gain and instant gratification.

Each plant and tree merges its energy together as its roots dig toward the heart of Gaia, while similarly, each human being merges their energy together as their Soul's light reaches toward the luminosity of Source. In between these realms, our hearts long to create heaven on earth. This is the vision our Souls hold as we create a New Earth: communities of light living gently on earth. The more people who come to realize this on an individual level, the more humanity will fulfill this on a global level. All you're responsible for is honoring your own wildhearted purpose in this moment.

Our bodies are born from Gaia and forever a part of Her, even in death. Gaia's health is our health; Her awakening is ours, too. In the undergrowth and overlights of life, we are all connected; this is where meaning is birthed.

If you don't know where to begin in the search for your life's purpose, consider how your life deepens in meaning and significance when you are intertwined with other people and nature. You have a way of intuitively lightening the load for others when you are gathered with them. Summon a vision of yourself in community, connected to the land, sharing your ample gifts, and being lifted higher from each meaningful experience. Remember … *purpose grows where meaning flows.*

Begin there, then go deeper.

· PRACTICE ·
Inner Compass Soul Prompts

Meaning shows up in life in many ways; its presence is always grounded, sure, and valuable. Here are some prompts for you to explore in your journal to discover more about what brings meaning to your purpose and depth to your life.

- Deep within the compass of your heart lives a magnet that consistently steers you toward your highest purpose. Where do you see that pointing to in this moment? Write down whatever comes to your mind, no matter how subtle or irrational it seems. How can you describe that direction? What will you do to follow your heart?

- What opens you up to your inner sense of meaning each day? When you look back over the way your purpose has evolved over the last few years, what were the highlights that lit you up from within? How do you make this planet a better place? (Because you *genuinely* do.) Write down these answers from your Higher Self if you struggle to answer them from your human self.

- Think of a time when you connected with nature and you felt like you were positively contributing. Tune in to the energy of your heart and feel what that moment was like for you. You may see visions, hear words, or feel it in your body. Take note of this visceral exchange of energy and write down the answers to these questions: What did you give of yourself as a contribution? Why did it feel so meaningfully good? What did you receive in return? Why was it important to receive this? How can you share of yourself more in this way?

THE JOY OF CREATING IN THE DESERT

There will be times in life when you're facing a blank canvas, a wide-open field, an empty planner. New beginnings, fresh starts, and infinite opportunities can be exciting or daunting. You may feel unprepared, but your heart knows the way; it cleared the decks for a reason. Begin, and you will soon discover the strength of assurance in each heartfelt step you take.

• JOURNEY •
Open Spaces and Inspired Visions

Imagine yourself immersed in the fields you call home, when you discover a patch of land that inspires a new inner vision to come to life. You want to work with the land, but you're waiting for the right timing, the prompts in your dreams, and the aligned connection between you and the earth.

You experience such excitement with every space, not because you want to change everything in nature, but because in the process of collaboration with the land, you feel in touch with your purpose and with the joy of service.

Nature shows her intention and preferences to you clearly when you show up in this state of appreciation and creativity. Some areas of the land wish to be kept bare and open, while others crave more trees and plants. There are places that show you the potential of a food forest, syntropic farming, or a wildflower landscape; others open themselves up to ponds, play areas, or sacred spaces. The visions are always unique, full of character and unexpected details, enlivening you with anticipation.

On the days when your heart is so deeply intertwined with Mama Gaia, you feel Her breathe through you, you hear Her wisdom as yours, and your hands move in ways that tend to you and the land with such delicate strength and intuitive knowing.

EVERY LIFE IS A CREATIVE ACT

I believe everyone is creative, but not everyone has an artistic calling. I don't paint or draw often, but I sing and play my drum, design luminous collages, plant tropical flowers, write incessantly, redesign my house often, and make up games with my kids. And as soon as I put together a vision board, my life blows open and becomes the most colorful playground imaginable.

For me, a vision board starts with a blank piece of cardboard or a cork pinboard and a pile of scrap paper from my favorite magazines. I love the nothingness in the beginning; it excites me. With a cup of cacao, a stick of glue or a jar of pins, and playful music, something uniquely inspiring and deeply creative comes alive from nothing.

When you allow your desires and ideas to take a visionary form on paper, your subconscious mind brings this vision board to life. It seemingly comes from nowhere, like a magical oasis in the desert.

The magic is *you*.

As the process unfolds intuitively, what comes together is a layered, multifaceted, wildhearted vision from a handful of images, emotions, ideas, dreams, and destinies.

The inspiration is amplified with patient spaciousness, a creative heartspace, a joyful mindset, and materials that lift you higher into your purpose, high above what your humanness might think is possible.

Open spaces can be terrifying. Some people look at a blank piece of paper and find it difficult to write anything. They freeze. Others are concerned about getting it wrong or messing it up or not looking as creative as someone else. They procrastinate. The brilliant thing about creativity it that you can't get it wrong, there's no way to mess it up (mess is usually the point), and by comparing it with someone else's creation, you're creating from an external viewpoint rather than from the wellspring within.

I look at the vision board above my computer screen many times a day as I sit down to write, play, design, create, connect, and eat chocolate. There are no words on my board, only layer upon layer of beautiful images. These images are more powerful together as they shape the course of my life.

Images and visions play an important role in bringing to life our blueprint of light. The intuitive heart that guides us along our journey is so deeply entwined with the visual, dreamy subconscious mind. When our physical senses bring information into our being, this goes straight into our subconscious, which then sends small amounts of information to the conscious mind (we are only conscious—or aware—of small amounts of information in any moment), while most of the sensory input gets tucked away into the subconscious or unconscious minds. It's the subconscious mind that steers our intuition through visions, images, dreams, feelings, and sensations. Words can't sink below the conscious mind into the powerfully creative subconscious mind, so I keep them away from vision boards.

Looking at a vision board with gratitude is a powerful habit for creating a purpose that fills you with joy and contentment. Seen each day, the images will soak right into your heart, the portal to your subconscious, informing your intuitive self that you are already living the life of your dreams. Your being doesn't know the difference between the images on your vision board or the other "real" scenes you look at in your life. It accepts all as your reality and then creates more of it, depending on your emotions, feelings, and thoughts.

That's why it's so important to play in the desert. To start from scratch. To meditate on the dark space of nothing and let the stars land where they will.

Every precious life is a creative act.

Some of my greatest ideas have arrived during a break from social media and writing, when I've sat on the beach for a day or two or taken myself and a good book to a cabin in the woods. It's only a metaphorical desert, but it's a healing, expansive, quiet space to sink into nothingness and welcome serendipity.

Your purpose is as much about reveling in the abundant, lush flora on your path as it is about dancing through the sandy desert with seemingly nothing around you other than a blank canvas of opportunity.

· RITUAL ·

Create Your Own Magnetic Vision Board

Having a vision board is a beautiful way of manifesting the life you desire. Here is my process for bringing the magic together.

1. Decide where you want your vision board to live. Will it be most inspiring on an altar, up on a wall, next to a mirror, behind a cupboard door, above your computer, or on the fridge? Choose a place you look at often.

2. Start with a large, thick piece of cardboard or cork-
    board that's the right size for your space. White or
    black are great background options for a variety of
    visuals, but the color choice, decoration, and frame
    are completely up to you.

3. Set an intention for the vision board. Would you like
    to feel invigorated and happy? Are you calling in a new
    career? Are you showcasing aspects of your current job
    on a higher level of awareness? Are you using it to have
    fun and play? Write this down on a piece of paper and
    stick to the back of the board where you won't see it; it
    will infuse the overall vision with your intention.

4. Grab a pile of old magazines you've finished read-
    ing or buy some from a secondhand store or online.
    Decide on an overall feel, essence, or color theme and
    cut out images from the magazine. I'd recommend
    not adding words to the vision board because this
    usually means the conscious mind gets too involved,
    and the heartfelt, magical imagery is lost a little. But
    if there are a couple of words you want to cut out or
    write down, try it out and see how they work with the
    visuals.

5. Place the images all over your board to create a draft
    vision, adjust until it feels aligned, then start gluing
    or pinning your images down. Any leftover pictures
    can go into the picture slot in your wallet, a small
    frame elsewhere in your home, or a creative card for
    a friend.

6. Look at it each day with gratitude and bless the vision
    to your life.

7. When your vision board begins to feel uninspiring, it may be that you've achieved what you needed it for. Adjust the images or start again to freshen it up. If starting again, cleanse the board and set a fresh intention.

Now that you have a visual creation that connects you to the slipstream of dreams in your heart, it's time to deepen your connection to who you are among this magnificent vision.

Chapter 2

CREATIVELY
EQUIP YOURSELF

*"Creativity occurs in the moment,
and in the moment we are timeless."*[3]
— JULIA CAMERON

You already have all you need to pursue the dreams of your heart. You were born with gifts that are as bright and ancient as your Soul, and you've cultivated and strengthened your talents intuitively with every job and experience. You already have what you need, and if you're facing in the direction of your heart, you're ready to take the next step.

There will occasionally be moments and opportunities that call for a deeper connection to the medicine you've already brought with you in this lifetime. This connection can be found in a mentor, guide, or teacher; in a course, diploma, or degree; in travel, experience, or training.

No one else can tell you precisely what to do with your precious life, but there are those who created a Soul contract with you to assist you at certain points, as you do for others. Living a life

---

3. Julia Cameron, *The Artist's Way: A Spiritual Path to Higher Creativity* (New York: J. P. Tarcher/Putnam, 1992), 139.

of wildhearted purpose is about balancing your sovereign inner knowing and resolve with the support and inspiration of those you walk beside.

In this chapter, you'll sharpen your vision for your purpose so you can see how remarkably equipped you already are, how to honor your authenticity, how to share your Soul's medicine, and what success means to you.

ANCIENT SKILLS, TOOLS, AND TEACHERS

You have an extensive array of gifts within your being—many, you've been creating and nourishing for lifetimes. Envisioning your dreams calls on these gifts to be remembered and revealed; living your wild purpose calls for them to be embodied in this life.

· JOURNEY ·
Stretching Your Wings, Softening Your Light

See yourself on the next stretch of your journey waking in the morning, feeling softer than usual. There's an ache within your sorrowful heart and a knowing in the middle of the ache.

As you take your morning walk to collect food for the day, you feel weaker than normal. Your heart is guiding you to go gently; your legs call you to stay close to your tent. All along your journey, you've met many wise friends and masters who have shared their wisdom with you. You've tucked all these messages into your inner heart's pocket, saving them for whenever they may be needed. Today feels like a good day to slow down, follow the surrender of your body, and recall the words of the wise.

When you've finished breakfast, your legs move slowly toward the firepit you set up a few days ago. Intuitively collecting some warm ash from last night's fire, you pack it into a jar for later. You start up a small, fresh fire to boil some water, then pour the water into a tea of dried herbs you've been told by local elders have deep healing properties. As you sip this delicate medicine, you notice an unusual shape in the periphery of the small clearing. Moving closer, you see it's a barn owl lying on the ground. Her spirit has passed on to another realm and is asking you to be the caretaker of her soft and weightless body. You bow to bless her Soul, sending it to Source with infinite blessings for her next life and beyond. Then you set her precious body on a pile of grass and, retrieving the few tools you own from your bag, work gently with the ancient skills of your Soul. Your body remembers how to remove wings and preserve other parts of this precious animal; your mind can barely keep up, though you learn soon enough, it doesn't have to.

With wings stretched, salted, covered, and drying in the sun, other parts covered in salt, and the rest of the body wrapped in flowers and buried with love, you sit nearby to meditate on your health and the reason for this owl's visit. You meet with the owl's spirit, who tells you her body was given to you to activate your ancient skills and to heal your heavy heart, which is causing your body to ache. With her radiant eyes of limitless vision, she sees all the way into your being. She knows the bright expanse of your love and the sadness you feel at times when you're alone, carving your life without anyone to cocreate with or lean on for support.

Your tears flow unabated; your gratitude, with them. You sit in meditation for most of the day, guided by this tender and wise owl spirit to heal emotions you've hidden for so long. You take a long break for dinner and stretching, then, guided by your own soft body, clear mind, and empowered spirit, you lie on the grass. Rubbing ash into your heartspace to represent fire, embracing the earth that holds you strong, shoulders covered with two large wings connected intimately to air, and tears flowing from the well of salt water within, you open your field to the stars, nature beings, birds, and elements to heal and connect to a new understanding of your wisdom and power.

You lie there for the rest of the evening, breathing deeply into your being, calling on light, and praying to be healed and whole. After a while, once the tears dry, you begin to laugh. Your belly shakes with gentle relief; a transformation has occurred. The Masters and Shamans you've met on your journeys were right; now your gifts are ready to be shared.

As you sit and place the wings by your side, you call on the owl spirit to stay with you and show you a higher vision for your life. With a heart as soft and light as a feather, you roll into bed, feeling less alone than ever, and knowing your dreams will be full of radiant guidance from above.

MERGING ANCIENT SKILLS WITH MODERN INTUITION

The way I envisage the future, this glorious New Age we are creating together, is that we are to live more immersed than ever in nature. No matter how guided we are by our clever minds and light speed technology, we need to live on earth with deep reverence for the natural space and lively elements we call home. I sense a global movement away from impassive bright city lights onto more expansive land where we can once again witness the stars in all their radiance and follow the cues of the seasons more intimately.

For thousands of years we have taken Her for granted, our Mother Gaia. We've stripped Her of Her glorious beings, dug greedy holes into Her sides, polluted Her aura, sprayed Her medicine with toxins, and denied Her ultimate power.

This journey into a New Earth will require that we love Her with everything we've got.

To work in Her service, we need to remember our own ancient skills—the ones we've been working on for lifetimes—as well as connect with teachers who live in service to Her. It matters who we learn from and how we stay aligned with what our heart desires. We are all students, teachers, and mentors. All of us.

Mother Nature is the ultimate alchemist for *merging our ancient skills with our modern intuition.*

You can learn from a colony of ants or the wisest guru. You can meditate with a tree or learn from a university. You can study endlessly at colleges because that's what lights you up, or you can surf the ecstatic waves of the ocean and learn from the energy that swirls beneath. All of life has the capacity to teach you and inspire the greatest vision for your life.

You will never stop learning, but that doesn't mean you are lacking; you are *remembering.*

There's no charted hierarchy or perfect algorithm to learning; just listen to your greatest teacher, your heart. Your heart might nudge you toward a PhD, a cabin near a mountain, a sacred healing circle, or a wildlife sanctuary. Your lessons will never stop teaching you, your teachers will never stop calling you, your wisdom has been with you since birth, and your students are ready when you are.

If you create a life of balance between learning, teaching, waiting, integrating, doing, and being, you will feel the symbiotic nature of life move through you, keeping you alert, grateful, valued, empowered, and humble in your wisdom. If you spend too much time learning, which can be vital at the beginning of any adventure, then you may feel stuck, unable to dream, create, or serve. If you lean into teaching too much, you may topple over with the weight of all you give to others. Learn when you can, teach what you know, share mindfully in humility.

Your life will lead you right into the sage and loving field of those who are predestined to guide you. Those who are fated to walk beside you, share their stories with you, light a fire for you, and empower you will be there in perfect timing, just as you need them. Those who are not for you will feel out of sync with love. They may hurry you into making a decision, they may cling to a certain superiority, they may not welcome your questions, or perhaps everything about them looks and sounds ideal but your heart whispers *no, no, no*.

Your teachers will have much to say, but equally they will know when to listen, how to hold space for you, and when to walk away. You may find your teachers in an ashram, on a bus, at a retreat, in a healing setting, in a relationship, at college, in a job, or as a mentor or coach. They may be a lifelong friend or an hour of connection.

The true nature of any wisdom exchange is one of the most important reasons we incarnated on this planet: to connect and grow with each other. As we do this, our vision expands, deepens, and comes to life. We see our potential in the eyes of another.

The skills you pick up along the way are often ancient skills you're remembering and implementing in this life. When you *merge your ancient skills and modern intuition*, they become an asset for you and your community as well as for the highest well-being of Mother Earth. That's when you know you are absolutely living on purpose.

Don't let your ego trick you into thinking that everything you do with your skills must make money or have a big reach. Carving a statue out of stone has a perfect purpose within itself, even if you don't sell it. Making a delicious meal from scratch has a deeply profound purpose, even if it's just for you. Planting an herb garden is purposeful; so is creating a personal altar, humming in the shower, framing your favorite photos, decorating your space with love, and watching inspiring documentaries. Everything in your daily life doesn't have to be purposeful in the egoic sense—financially fruitful or striving to be better than yesterday. Your life needs only to be of service to the powerful and mysterious path of your heart. This may bring you endless financial abundance or a sense of mastery, or this may make you well known. Or it may lead to a humble and simple life. All are abundantly beautiful.

You will inevitably rediscover your ancient skills, develop your most potent talents, and find your greatest teachers right when you need them. Have no doubt. The Universe wants you living your dreams in the most abundant ways and will bring you exactly what you need along the way.

You may have a vision of these teachers before you meet them, or it may be a spontaneous meeting of hearts that opens you up to a more defined vision for your life. And that's what teachers are for: to help us see the sparks of possibility in the hidden depths of our being.

· PRACTICE ·
Teacher Guru Soul Prompts

I love to ask friends for advice, and I have a handful of mentors I reach out to whenever I need them. It's not easy for me to ask for help; I don't even like reading user guides for *anything* I buy. But when it comes to my purpose, I appreciate a fresh perspective from someone who can envisage my journey in ways I simply cannot.

If you don't have anyone you would call a teacher or mentor, or you've outgrown your previous teachers and you'd like to bring a new, inspired guide into your life, take out your journal and write a letter to them, asking them to make themselves known in your life.

Write down in detail the kind of person you would like to connect with and how you want to feel when working with them. Here are three examples.

1. I call in to my life a divinely feminine and intuitively empowered mentor who helps me feel soft, courageous, expansive, and creative.

2. I am grateful for the arrival of a guide who inspires me to live as the highest version of me every day through daily rituals, loving thoughts, and healthy habits.

3. I now open to connect with a teacher grounded in their divine masculine energy who will show me how to heal all blocks to abundance and open my heart to receiving all that is meant for me.

In life, it's good to have a balance of inner and outer, masculine and feminine, creative and logical advice. When you feel like reaching into the sacred chambers of your own heart for wisdom, call on your inner guru. Give them a name, if you like. Ask them questions and write down answers as they flow to you.

Know that all wisdom, all healing, all activation essentially comes from within. Everything you "receive" from another person is simply a remembering and recalibration of your perfection, your wholeness, your knowing, your multidimensional being. You've already got this, but it's so worthwhile to be reminded and inspired.

OWN YOUR UNIQUENESS AND
SPIRITED AUTHENTICITY

The more you follow your willful heart, the more you'll notice that not everyone agrees with you or wants to join or support you on your quests. As you deepen your call to authenticity, you'll know that it doesn't matter how many people are close by on your journeys; it's the quality of companionship by your side that matters.

· JOURNEY ·
Following the Slipstream

Glimpse yourself stepping out of your tent earlier than normal, catching an early morning star. With a prayer for protection and guidance, you pack your tent, give thanks to the owl and earth for holding you in your dreams, and begin walking the next part of your journey.

In tune with your strong inner compass, you follow the lyrical voice of love along rambling routes between trees, over lakes, and around mountains, humming the song of the earth as She pulses through the soles of your feet.

In an unanticipated moment, a friend comes toward you. You hug them fervently, grateful for the exchange of warmth, share a few words about your respective journeys, and continue in opposite directions. Soon a few more acquaintances come toward you. After hugs and meaningful exchanges, you notice that this stretch of your journey has a slightly worn path, unlike the bowed grasses and strewn logs you're used to; many have walked this passage before you. More people come your way; some ask if you'll join them, keen to have your high vibrancy with them. Others nod knowingly, honoring your heart.

You pause and consider the flow of people moving, like a sea of connectivity and light, all for a cause you and your heart aren't in sync with. They sing an unfamiliar song, move toward an unknown goal, and, for a moment, you feel lost and confused. Your outer senses latch on to the river of people rushing past, and you forget the inner slipstream of your Soul's guidance.

When the majority has gone past, the sun comes out from behind a cloud, illuminating the pureness of your sight. The rays land on your feet, anchoring you into the dirt beneath you. Your inner knowing springs back to life, rekindling the certainty of your passageway.

Step by step you head uphill, smiling at those passing by, assured by the sun in all its brilliance that you are heading in the direction of your heart. As hunger stirs, nature provides food. As thirst beckons, a clear creek appears. Your every desire and need are taken care of.

As the sun begins to arc its descent, you look for a place to rest. Longing for community and connection but unable to resist the dream that takes you from the crowd, you come across a band of wild horses who invite you to stay. You find a sheltered space that feels like a sanctuary and put down your belongings. After you set up your tent, the horses invite you to roam the fields and find your evening meal.

All afternoon you explore the pasture with the speed and comfort of these beatific beasts. The strength of their movement deepens the pulse of your body. Their breath awakens a vital force within your lungs. Touching their necks with your bare hands reminds you of an ancient sensation of being one with the spirit of animals, of losing yourself in their presence, of complete trust and telepathy with all of nature.

After a meal in the woods, darkness settles, and the horses lead you back to your camping spot for the night. As you approach, you hear a sound that vibrates through your being and uplifts every cell.

It's the sound of community and fire, of Soul's song and laughter. The closer you get, the brighter the reflection of flames in familiar eyes. Your family has found you. Although these are not the friends you saw today on the path, they are the Soul family you've been praying for. The Soul sisters and brothers who made a pact to reunite in this life. You've known this, seen this, heard this in your dreams. The horses knew it all along; they were an integral part of your Soul's journey.

Your Soul family was drawn along the magnetic pull of earth into your loving, aligned field according to the courageous and unconventional timelines you have each chosen.

You sink into this fellowship of rebellious grace, this web of incandescent light. In this blessed cradle you rest a while, day and night, for weeks on end, full of deep love, until your heart beckons you onward once again.

REBELLIOUS FAITH AND STUBBORN INTEGRITY

You are a rare and unique creature. Your Soul longs for the physical expression of a purpose destined long ago. That's why you're here, wandering the earth and these pages for the keys of discovery to visualize and create what you're here to do.

There will be times when you'll feel like you're heading in exactly the opposite direction to everyone around you. People you love and those who inspire you will walk toward and past you. Some of them may attempt to persuade you into their fold; others will acknowledge and support you on your way.

Remember, you and your brave Soul were never meant to follow anyone else's path. Each step you take in *rebellious faith* is grounded in the *stubborn integrity* of your authentic being.

Your purpose will, at times, feel isolating, lonely, selfish, prickly, testing, and wearisome. But if you follow your rebel spirit, it will ultimately feel magical, incomparable, breathtaking, aligned, serendipitous, mysterious, and brave.

The only way to fully illuminate your unique vision is to follow your sovereign heart, and only your pure and sovereign heart. And it may seem ironic, but the more focused you are on creating magic from within rather than imitating what's around you, the more likely you are to find a close circle of friends: people who love, honor, accept, and celebrate you for all you are. They may sing a different song to you, but together your harmony is deep and exquisite. They may have different spiritual, philosophical, and sociological opinions and beliefs to you, but somehow your conversation is expansive, respectful, and inspiring. In fact, it's these conversations that equip you to discover your purpose; it's the insight that lands between the words that fuels your desires, activates your medicine, and excites your vision.

Communities, Soul family, beloved brothers and sisters will come and go. Let them. Open your heart to the flow of community; whoever is meant to be with you on your path will be there. They will find you no matter what.

I believe the greatest teachers and most important groups in our lifetime were prearranged perfectly before we all incarnated. At one timeless moment our Souls gathered together and set an intention and timeline for our inevitable reunion. We may have done this hundreds of times over our evolution together.

That's why you feel so at home and so unconditionally loved when you find your people. They can be part of an online group, a local community college, the people you work with, dance with, pray with, or walk with in nature. They know you by your light and aren't fazed by your darkness. They want the best and highest outcome for you.

They see, admire, and praise your *rebellious faith and stubborn integrity.*

If you live in an area where you aren't celebrated by your neighbors, where you feel awkward doing things differently to everyone else, then you might consider moving to an area where the locals are more like-minded and kindhearted—not so that everyone agrees with you, but so that you can feel more at home in your surroundings and bloom vigorously in that space.

The people who live in your apartment block or in the houses on your street will impact you through the energy they emanate. Even if you never communicate with them in person, your energy is feeling theirs, and their energy is sensing yours, too. If the street you live on has a median vibration that pulses out waves of despair, anger, or confusion, that will impact you and your energy. You can wake each day and rise above it, you can live with a white light shield around your place, you can hum mantras to ward it off all day, but it still cannot possibly be the best place for you to sleep, rest, eat, work, and play. Living in an area that resonates around the higher vibrations of courage, hope, and acceptance will create greater ease in your home, the food you grow will be wonderfully healthy, you will have inspiring conversations often, and your purpose will be more palpable to envisage and easier to express.

Whether you're in a big city or a small country town, an aligned community will provide a place of rest and song. *They* are the people who are craving your gifts. *They* want you to live your wildest purpose. The *connection* you have with each person will be your purpose, whether it looks like it's connected to your work or not.

If you're lost in the sea of your shadow, insecurities, trauma, or other inhibitions, you may lose sight of your community for a while, or they may move onto another path without you. This happens to most seekers on their journey and is a sign that it's time to retreat and heal. You haven't done anything wrong—you *cannot* do anything wrong. You're simply being shown that there is healing to be done and compassion to be given generously to yourself. There's no need to catch up with others; this isn't a race. When the healing is done, those you need will come effortlessly into your realm.

If there comes a time when your lengthy loneliness or quiet disheartenment sees you fall into the arms of a group that doesn't want the best for you, walk away without fuss, sending them love and blessings on the way out. You'll know they're not your people because you'll feel unheard, confused, edgy, unaccepted, mistreated, or used.

Keep walking your untamed path. Revel in the mystery of community. Some communities may last decades or a lifetime, others a weekend. Stay true to your unique self and blissful connections will find their way to you.

· Practice ·
Calling In Community Soul Prompts

I believe it's so important to consciously create the kind of community our hearts are longing for. Community can be our neighbors, colleagues, or extended family. It can be the like-hearted people we meet at our local school, community gardens, food markets, creative gatherings, soulful workshops, or sacred circles, or simply those we handpick.

The intention behind these journal prompts is to remind you of your Soul family, the ones you feel most sublimely at home with, and to call more of them in. Answer the questions that speak to where you're at with your community.

- If you are part of a small or large Soul family or community, write down what it is about them that you're grateful for. The more detailed you are about the specific blessings your Soul sisters and brothers bring into your life, the more you will notice them, show gratitude for them, and allow these and other blessings to richly flow to you from your community and elsewhere.

- As you reflect on your community, write a little about those who have been difficult to deal with. Shower them with compassion as this will help them on their path and make it easier for you to be around them.

- While an open heart and endless warmth will be helpful as you navigate life within your community, you will also require firm boundaries around communication and behavior that aren't tolerable or healthy. There's no need to focus on what isn't favorable in your eyes; rather, know and trust that your gut will tell you when something isn't right, and your wise heart will show you how to tend to the unease. Write down what boundaries you're ready to put into place and what other steps you need to take: perhaps a one-on-one chat, a group conversation, or leaving the community, vicinity, or group for a short time.

- If you are still searching for your community, write down twelve words of intention for calling them closer to you, such as *support, love,* and *generosity.* Then activate these words by writing or saying, "With these words I call in my community according to my highest good. I gratefully welcome a supportive community of brothers and sisters who appreciate and love me for who I am. I am willing to serve my community with my gifts and generosity, as well as receive from them. And so it is." With your inner eye open, see them coming to you clearly in a vision; feel them tangibly in your realm as an important part of your purpose that you desire to connect with.

- Finally, write down how your current community or friends inspire your purpose. Look at a few of the most important connections around you and note how they have enhanced your connection to your inner calling.

ILLUMINATE YOUR INIMITABLE SOUL MEDICINE

Source light is like an invisible sun that has no end, its rays pulsing through all of life's incarnations as earthly or otherworldly beings. As the Source light of our Soul merges with the form of our body, we become a rare creature. There is no one like you on this planet or any other, at this time or any other past or future time. No two bees are the same; no daisy is ever repeated. We are all perfect, exquisite, remarkably exclusive beings with a purpose like no other.

· JOURNEY ·

Always Connected, Forever Unique

Envisage a sublimely gentle dragonfly following you. It floats above you during your pauses to take in a sunrise, rest by a tree, and eat leisurely. The buzz of its wings is like rustling bamboo, soothing and awakening your senses.

One afternoon as you swim naked in a gentle creek, feeling revived and sensual, you find yourself surrounded by four dragonflies colored red, orange, blue, and purple. As the water calms your whole body, the sound of these ancient insects settles your mind. Lying against a rock halfway submerged in the creek in the golden afternoon sun, you witness a series of images flash before you, like mirages over the meandering water.

Each vision tells a story with you as the main character, only you look different in each story. After a while, you notice a thread running through them all: the presence of your Soul. This revelation of your Soul's unique disposition delights you in this appearance of past lives. Intrigued, you ask to be shown more lives where your gifts were animated and shared.

Life after life flows past your awareness, thread after thread catches your attention. As the visions begin to fade and your mind grows in clarity, you realize with startling sensitivity that the gifts that have started to reveal themselves to you in this life have been the same in all the lives you saw. You feel a new connection to your Soul; this striking perception has tilted your reality, and you feel more grounded in this life and your purpose.

The dragonflies come closer. Closing your eyes a little, you feel a golden thread illuminate your Soul all the way back through thousands of past lives to your birth from Source.

In your mind's eye, you see how everyone is connected with such a thread that connects them to Source. And given how connected all beings are in the Universe, the web of light is, as far as you can see, the most real aspect of life itself.

Each person weaves their light, their Soul's innate and powerful medicine, from lifetime to lifetime. Healing bodies, saving lives, holding space, reviving love, birthing creativity, and inspiring wholeness. Their light meets with other lights, illuminating aspects in each other. Our light contains the medicine for each life and, depending on our Soul's progress, is the catalyst for the blueprint coming to life in each incarnation.

Seeing this from such a vast perspective shows you how in every single moment we are living, breathing beings of precise medicine and vital purpose. Always connected to our source, *the Source*.

When you open your eyes, the dragonflies have flown away, and the stars are beginning to emanate, one by one, through the inky expanse above. You wrap yourself in warm clothes and give thanks for the journey of the master dragonflies.

YOUR UNIQUELY POWERFUL SOUL MEDICINE

We *all* have *uniquely powerful Soul medicine* within us. It seems contradictory, impossible even, for every single human being on earth to be unique, but we are. Extraordinarily so.

No two fingerprints, crystals, flames, snowflakes, or feathers are exactly alike. No two hearts beat to the same drum. No two voices sing the same note. And no two humans will ever have exactly identical callings.

When you get to know yourself deeply—through loving self-exploration and in the reflections of your relationships—you will become attuned to your ancient nuances.

As a psychic, I'm often guided by symbology, and I pass what I see on to friends, family, and clients. Symbols are brilliant because they surpass language and are exquisitely simple. I can share them with my children in the same way I pass them to a dear friend or someone I know nothing about, and they will *always* resonate. I appreciate it when visions, symbols, and colors show up in meditations because I am a symbol-loving, visual clairvoyant who sees light beings as colorful orbs often.

As a meditative guide, I love taking clients and groups on intuitively navigated and deeply moving visual journeys to explore, understand, and heal their inner realms. It's such perfect medicine for me to share because it brings together the visual aspect of my gifts as well as the storytelling. When different aspects of my gifts and talents are woven together to create an offering, I feel bliss and satisfaction each time I'm in that process.

This is my *uniquely powerful Soul medicine.*

If I attempt to serve others in any way that doesn't come from the light of my being, the Soul medicine deep within, then I feel misaligned. If I do something solely because other people think I should, or someone else is doing it and making it look good, especially if I haven't checked in with my heart, then it won't resonate with others or feel exciting for me.

Before I knew myself at this level, I often felt like an imposter. And I believe that's what imposter syndrome really is—a feeling of disconnection from our truth, gifts, talents, wisdom, confidence, and expression. When we know ourselves and are comfortable being seen and received for who we are, we no longer need to hide behind the façade of a character that isn't representative of who we really are. Through self-knowing, we learn to allow the medicine to flow naturally.

The word *medicine* comes from Latin *medicina*: "a healing art; remedy." There are many remedies to help us when we're out of balance, but when it comes to your purpose, there's no need to search for a healing art outside of yourself. By being true to you, *you are the remedy*.

To know intimately your Soul's own medicine, the salve you share with others, and to connect with your gifts and talents on the deepest level, you need to get to know the Universe within you. While this can be confronting for some and playful for others, it doesn't have to be stressful.

It's as simple as being with yourself more.

When you're curious and present to the multifaceted creature that you are, you'll begin to see how you show up in ways that love and serve others. Perhaps it's in the way you consciously cook or create luscious tea ceremonies. It could be the way your hands seem to radiate healing energy or how your listening helps others feel at peace. Maybe it's the way you decorate homes to feel warm and cozy or how easily you read the passage of the heavenly stars.

Knowing yourself will help you sense the medicine that naturally pours from your being every day. Once known, this medicine can be shaped lovingly to increase its potency, direct its light, and open your life to shared abundance.

You are the center of the vision you're creating for your purpose. Radiating from the core of *you* is your *uniquely powerful Soul medicine*; it's an intrinsic part of who you are.

When you get to know yourself better, you will find that your medicine goes beyond words—it's your wordless presence. If you could look into the light beams of your presence, you'd see your gifts and talents radiating through.

Your *gifts* are the medicine you bring into this life from when your Soul was first birthed from Source. Within your Soul are many gifts, active from birth or activated during life—the golden thread that laces all past and future lives together.

Thanks to the process of past-life regression, I've been able to revisit many of my past lives and see the golden thread that is common among many. I can see that I've been a spirited healer, empowered writer, and wildhearted rebel in numerous lives. Knowing this has been more than interesting, it's been important to the development of my skills and confidence in these areas in this particular incarnation.

Your *talents* are the skills, brilliance, and strengths you've developed throughout this life. Talent goes beyond what you excel at in all levels of education and employment and extends out to experience in all forms.

Gifts and talents aren't always easy to separate and analyze. They blend beautifully together in your purpose as you live as a harmonious whole. There are a handful of prompts below to help you understand them better. Just know that you came into this life already blessed with potent gifts, and no matter what your life looks like now, you are talented beyond measure. As you deepen your knowledge of your sacred gifts and intuitive talents, you will more easily and viscerally color the vision that your Soul is calling you toward.

Your gifts are ancient, your talents are endless, and your Soul's medicine is radically unique.

• PRACTICE •
Know Your Medicine Soul Prompts

Besides spending more time simply and lovingly reflecting on who you are during quiet meditations, daily routines, and curious conversations with others, there are ways to consciously discover yourself in detail in your journal through the questions below. Have a glimpse at the following prompts and answer them positively from the heart without overthinking the process.

- How do people feel when they meet you for the first time? What is their energetic reaction to simply being with you? How do friends react when they see you?

- In what ways did you interact with the outdoors as a child that felt fun, healing, and natural? Where was your favorite place to go? What simple ways did you engage with animals, insects, trees, flowers, rocks, waterways, and sunshine? What was it about nature that helped you feel better?

- When you're looking for ideas or creative inspiration, where do you go? Do you look to the stars, sit on a rock, climb a tree, talk to grasshoppers, play with a cat or dog, go for a forest walk, swim at the beach, or pick flowers? What in nature helps you feel most expansive and inspired?

- What's your initial reaction to a friend who is sick and needs help? Is it to cook for them, clean their abode, send healing energy, take them to appointments, or sit with them and listen? How do you take care of others who are feeling down? Do you give them advice, organize help, make them a cup of tea, offer them a massage, give them a gift voucher for a day spa, or hug them endlessly? Write down in detail what you do for loved ones; this is an aspect of your purpose that can be amplified in your life.

- What's your dream job? Detail the kind of job you'd never want a holiday from. Where is it located, who are you working with, what are you doing each day, how much do you get paid, and how are you being of service? As you write this down, be specific and detailed, keep it real and dreamy, feel excited and grounded, and *know* that it's possible.

- When you have a quiet day at home with no work, cleaning, or cooking to do, what do you like to do? What makes you happiest? Why? How would this make you feel?

- If someone gifted you with an empty shop or studio, what would you set up there? What would be your role? How would it help the local community? What would be your medicine? It could be a retail space, healing center, or anything that inspires you. Draw the space if you like, and if this is something you're inspired to create in your life, make a clear, colorful, descriptive layout.

- What gifts do you believe you're carrying with you, like a golden thread through ancient lifetimes? What were you good at as a child without any previous experience? What comes naturally to you that benefits others?

- What talents have you been working on in this lifetime? What have you studied and worked on that feels intuitively strong? What jobs have you had where you felt like you had a sixth sense built into your human capabilities?

Now that you've answered these, look through your notes and see what you can discover about yourself and your medicine. Notice how these insights create a more textural and tangible vision for your purpose.

REDEFINE SUCCESS WITH SOVEREIGNTY

We're conditioned to expect success to look like ribbons and stickers, toys and rewards, money and cars, flattery and promotions. But when we follow the way of our heart, we know that the warmth of the morning sun and the radiance of the stars each night—with a few hugs in between—are the greatest success.

· JOURNEY ·
Honoring the Unquiet Nudge

Imagine the sensation of restlessness after being in the same place for a while; you're ready for a fresh spark of adventure. It's the end of fall, and you're sensing a more internal focus in your routine. This self-reflection is causing you to notice and surrender what doesn't feel in harmony with your heart.

You've noticed a resentment lurking within you, a hangover from your earlier life when you were rewarded constantly with flattery and money, compliments and invitations, rewards and celebrations, which have almost vanished completely.

As you move on, you're distracted. A part of you is searching to fill this painful hole within. You haven't learned fully or trusted completely that all the abundance and love is already, always with you.

You come across a plateau of rocks shimmering in the midday sun. One rock in particular shimmers so bright that you stoop to take a closer look. Up close, you notice how brightly it glistens—impossibly so. There's no easy way to lift the rock out of the earth, so you ditch your pack, grab your tools and a few solid branches from the woods nearby, and start breaking up the rock. Your heart aches each time you strike at the rock, your curiosity turns to greed, your arms ache at the exertion, but you go on, ignoring your body and following the egoic commands of your mind.

When you're on the verge of giving up, wondering if the whole scheme is worth it, suddenly the rock cracks into a thousand tiny pieces. As you bend down, scrambling foolishly for precious crystals, a large red ant bites your ankle. Yelling and pounding your fist in pain, you realize how irresponsible you've been. Taking a break to heal your painfully swollen foot, you notice the golden rock from a lower angle, and you realize the shimmer was only on the dew-covered surface in the morning sun.

Humbled by this misadventure, you place all the broken pieces of rock back in the large crater you created and hobble into the woods to form an apology fit for Goddess Gaia. You collect flowers and feathers, pebbles and leaves, and fuse together an offering. Infusing it with prayers of gratitude and asking for forgiveness, you take it to the broken rock, like a wreath bestowed on the broken crown of a queen.

As you sit next to the rock, tears of grief and pain intermingling, the voice of Gaia speaks through your heart:

Dear One, you have been conditioned to overlook the wildly abundant nature of your own being. You were taught to seek praise and rewards from others, when all along I was here, sharing my abundance with you every day, showering you with loving kindness, bathing you in complete adoration. Grieve your past; let it go. You're with me now; the Great Mother holds you close. With me, you are sovereign, victorious, successful, and blessed in every moment. I love you.

With deep and respectful appreciation, you head back to camp. It's dusk, and you're exhausted and hungry. Out of the woods emerges a friend; after many hugs, they tend to your foot, providing much-needed relief. While you are resting, they light a fire and make a simple dinner from the harvest in their bag. The conversation that ensues is ineffably heartening.

In this sacred moment of acquaintance, stars, and nourishment, you fathom how perfectly fulfilling life is when you live with an open and grateful heart.

YOU ARE INNATELY BOUNTIFUL

Taking responsibility for your actions and witnessing your impact on your community around you can be confronting at first, but it's ultimately the most mindfully satisfying way to live. While some people feel they need to take, conquer, and control to feel powerful, you have the power to change lives by simply *being* your bountiful, generous, lustrous self.

Working for other people, asking for promotions, driving a new car, and making loads of money are all well and good if the intention behind them is wholehearted, but having these as a primary focus can be limiting to the full expression of purpose. Embracing and sharing all your truth, love, and energy is a multidimensional experience, and one that shifts how you view success. Constantly striving for success means you never feel successful; knowing that success is part of who you are means you are free to give and receive abundantly at all times.

As a sovereign being, you do not need the permission or direction of another; these can only come from the sacred inner sanctum of your heart.

I believe all human beings are on a spiritual journey toward peace and love. Many have been sidetracked, derailed by trauma, greed, or interference, and strayed off their path. Some don't want to know about their wild ways, and others will find them later in life.

But deep down we all yearn to love and be loved, to live in peace and harmony, and to have the freedom to choose how we do this. When peace is the goal, rather than surging wealth or a glamorized ego, the goal posts for success become inward, rather than outward, and we live more mindfully, grateful for each moment, no matter how it looks. We become more self-aware and naturally in tune with our purpose and community. We live lightly, connected to nature, with compassion for all. We feel sovereign in our being, unbound and untethered, able to create freely in a way that honors our supreme self. We touch on a profound feeling of success in rising early to catch a sunrise, singing with like-hearted friends, or creating with our hands. We become satisfied *in* the act of devoting ourselves to our work, not only when the work is done or rewarded. Through pure devotion, we feel the truth that *we are innately bountiful.*

Success will mean different things to everyone. It's supposed to. It's an empowering step to become conscious of what success feels like to you and allowing life to meet you there. As you create a vision for your life, as your purpose becomes louder within the beat of your heart, internalizing success, knowing what makes you feel sovereign, and looking to nature for wealth and health will empower you infinitely.

Simplify success for yourself. Reflect on each cycle with respect and reverence. Celebrate the long bath at the end of the day, the shell you find at the edge of the ocean, the belly laugh you have with a good friend, the book that brings lightness to your life, the creative collaboration you share with others, and all the understated moments of heaven on earth.

Learn about sovereignty; become conscious of who you give your power to and why. As you discover what makes you sovereign and trust yourself, you take your power back and naturally expect less praise, require fewer compliments, and lower your expectations of others.

You are already innately bountiful.

If you dare to make a momentous change to your life, love everyone and let go of *all* expectations. Lavish self-nurturing all over yourself each day. Fill yourself with the love and affection of nature. Feel sovereign and successful just as you are and watch how the Universe honors you wholly.

· PRACTICE ·
Manifesting Success Soul Prompts

I strongly believe in the power of affirmations to manifest greatness in life. We're all manifesting *something* with our thoughts each moment—we might as well make it amazing. This exercise works with the conscious mind to purposefully bring to life that which helps us feel fiercely successful. It requires complete honesty and will generate abundance in your life right where you want it the most. Here's how it works.

1. Take a full page in your journal and fill it with all the words that make you feel successful. Don't edit, judge, or censor yourself. When you feel complete, take a highlighter and circle the words that are most important to you.

2. Now, create three affirmations based on your top three words. Keep your affirmations positive and in the first person; for example, "My peace is my priority," "Success is an open heart," and "I open to the most lavish abundance that is meant for me."

3. You can create affirmations around anything you like; just be mindful of how you feel when you say them out loud. If they feel limiting, egoic, or untrue, consider more expansive, meaningful words that resonate with your heart. If they feel encouraging, confident, real, and abundant, you know you're onto a good selection.

4. Write these affirmations on a piece of paper and place them in your wallet, on your fridge, in your diary, or anywhere you look often. Say them out loud every day with a knowing smile. Allow abundance to flow to you and open to success in all its many wondrous forms.

Hold a vision of the highest, most bountiful success as already yours. Then surrender it all to love.

Chapter 3

DREAM WITH
THE ELEMENTS

*"The essence of wisdom is to be in harmony with nature, with the
natural rhythm of the universe. And whenever you are in harmony
with the natural rhythm of the universe you are a poet, you are a
painter, you are a musician, you are a dancer."*[4]

— OSHO

In this closing section of creating your vision for a purposeful
life, you'll be connecting to the elements of earth, wind, fire, and
water. Whenever you connect to the elements, you open to what
they have to teach you and how vibrantly alive they already are
within the Universe inside you.

Many people, especially in the West, believe the elements need
to be tamed for us to be safe. We yearn for softer waves, calmer
wind, fewer fires, and a stable earth. When we do this, we're not
only limiting the power of the elements, we're limiting our own
inherent, natural power. When we shift our outlook to appreciation, gratitude, and awe of the elements, we can expand exponentially as we commune with them heart-to-heart.

---

4.   Osho, *Creativity: Unleashing the Forces Within* (New York: Griffin, 1999), 36.

Mother Nature expresses Herself to us through the elements; they are in constant communication with our energy. The more we connect with the call of nature outside our homes, our cities, our smallness, our protective walls, and our screens, the more in tune with our inner nature we become. This is as much an inner journey as an outer one.

TRUST THE MAGNETIC PULL AND WISDOM OF LOVE

Your heart is a magnetic force, and each day the most powerful decision you can make is to allow that inner force to show you the truest vision of where to go. These visions from the heart are the pointed arrow of your Soul's loving compass.

· JOURNEY ·
Shapeshifting in the Depths

Sense what it might feel like to reemerge from the depths of winter into the sweet sunshine of early spring. After months of limited sun and clouded starlight, you are yearning for a warm adventure. You pack your bags, walk into the sunrise, and pause. In the stillness, you hear a voice that says *keep moving*. It's much less a loud directive and more of a loving impulse to move north.

As you move serendipitously, meandering through long, dry grass, you no longer feel lost. You're beginning to revel in a new state of ease with the unknown. You feel centered along an invisible stream of energy under your feet.

As you find your rhythm, the grass gradually turns into tall palm trees and flowering ginger. Humidity kisses your skin. Butterflies lap around frangipani trees. You hear a loud rushing noise and can't help but hurry toward it, curious beyond measure at what could possibly produce this kind of ecstatic sound.

The whirl of lifeforce energy that moves through you as you discover a waterfall flowing into a rocky plunge pool lifts the vibration of your being immeasurably. You feel completely alive, quenched by this divine offering. You take your clothes off, craving to be one with the water.

As you step into the luscious blues and greens, you sing with euphoria. You're overcome by the resounding energy around you and you lose all sense of yourself; your bodily boundaries vanish. You merge with the water, the rocks, the breeze, and the leaves raining gently around you. A loving, cosmic force moves through you, transforming every part of you. You close your eyes as you feel your shape shifting into a remarkably different expression.

Legs become a tail, torso ripples with gills, arms lengthen and lighten, eyes and nose metamorphose. Illuminated, you swim effortlessly to the depths under the waterfall's landing. The pull of your heart takes you behind the waterfall, into a dark cave that goes on for a soothing eternity. There is nothing to see, nothing to sense other than the coolness of the water on your scales and the slow and sure pulse within your center.

Love takes you on a journey you don't question or fear. As the dark encapsulates you, you awaken to the lights of your inner rainbow-hued cosmology. They shine bright, these guiding light codes within, their stunning phosphorescence reflecting on the cave walls. Soon your body moves downward, spiraling into the deep. Your breath lengthens and your eyes adjust effortlessly. In the cavernous surrounds, you catch a glimpse of a small light. Your vision springs to life, and you move toward it.

Swimming with intent, you become increasingly soft, open, and mindful. The light within this mystical treasure pulses from pink to red and back again. Over and over, mesmerizing your keen awareness. Intuitively, your hands reach out to hold it, but as soon as you touch it, it merges with you as light pulsing up your arms and into your heart.

Immediately the energy of your heart erupts, your inner core activated by the purest form of Love; all the colors of the rainbow—and some you've never witnessed before—fill the underwater abyss. The walls around you come to life, and you now recognize the curves and beams of this underwater temple. A home you once knew, once lived in, once loved.

Alive with the essence of Love, another creature comes into view. They swim toward you, their heart equally as open and charged, and more memories swarm through your conscious awareness. Visions of past lives together fill your inner sight. This radiant being smiles at you, takes your hands in theirs. They feel like an ancient Soul mate with a rich, shared star ancestry, having experienced many lives with you.

Together you swim back toward where you came. As you find your way past the waterfall and back onto the smoothness of warm rocks, you both shapeshift into the purely human forms you inhabit on land. Looking down at your body, familiar in many ways, you notice a striking new luminosity that permeates your skin and features.

Standing with your beloved, you bow before the water and the familiar depths of your ancient self. You gaze into the eyes of your love for a timeless moment. You feel so enormously grateful to have found your heart's mirror in the depths of Love.

THE LEY LINES OF LOVE

Love can be felt as the heart of Gaia, the energy of the Great Mother, the song of your heart, a high-vibrational frequency that guides you along the paths of your purpose and paints your sacred visions with you. It calls to you in many ways, but it always feels the same … *like home.*

Ley lines are invisible, linear contours underneath the surface of the earth that connect sacred sites. When seen from high above the earth, they are remarkably straight. They were first discovered (in the scientific sense) by Alfred Watkins in the 1920s while photographing landmarks in England, but they have always been understood and utilized by the Ancient Ones of this earth who've been attuned to the powerful portals of energy in specific points along the lines over many thousands of years.[5] Ancient temples, natural or made by humans, as monumental as the pyramids of Egypt or as humble as the dolmen of England, can be connected by unseen lines that hold high-vibrational energy.

The Chinese call them Dragon Lines, Australian Indigenous call them Songlines, and South American Shamans call them Spirit Lines. When viewed from space, they form a grid woven all over the earth. Where these lines meet, concentrated energy forms. These were the places where the Ancient Ones built sacred sites because of the spiritual power and augmentation of lifeforce. Naturally occurring sacred sites have formed at these intersecting points around earth, such as Uluru in the heart of Australia and Mount Shasta in California.

When we view our lives from above, we can see how our decisions have created a similar passage along *the ley lines of love's* deep and invisible energy. From this angle, we can see clearly the periods when we wandered away from truth and those spells when we trusted the magnetic flow.

5.   Alfred Watkins, *The Old Straight Track: Its Mounds, Beacons, Moats, Sites and Mark Stones* (Heritage Hunter, 2015).

When you tune in to the whispers, magic, signs, symbols, and direction of your heart, you will come back to the ley lines that form your inner blueprint.

If the ego rules the mind and your thoughts, love reigns supreme in your heart's chalice of emotions. Following the expansive, compassionate, joyous, and liberated threads of love are all you need to find your way. These threads pull you swiftly and softly into alignment.

Creating a vision for your life in tune with the higher emotions of peace, love, joy, hope, and bliss will take you along the highest possible timeline of each adventure in your life.

While timelines are connected to time and ley lines are connected to space, the lines of love's guidance within you are far more extraordinary and multidimensional than the human mind can fathom. Love goes beyond time and space to embrace *all* that you are. Love understands the uniquely infinite being you are; your mind can't do that. That's why the only way to feel into the magnetic pull of your purpose is to listen to your heart. It's the heart that speaks the language of love.

This is as ethereal as it is earthly.

We're all *electromagnetic* beings living on a vibrantly electromagnetic planet. Your iron-rich heart, the *magnetic* center of your body, pulses with the fluidity of blood that keeps you alive. Your body also has energy that flows along meridian lines and through neural pathways—these *electrical* currents keep you balanced, in communication, and healthy. The body of the earth circulates in a similar way. The ley lines that wrap around the earth's surface are the veritable meridian lines and neural pathways that circulate her powerful *electric* energy, while the rivers, oceans, and lava are the *magnetic*, life-giving arteries connected to Gaia's own iron-rich heart.

We are the earth; the earth is our body.

When we follow the wildhearted, electromagnetic nudges along our pilgrimage from one sacred moment of deep fulfillment, experience of bliss, or purposeful connection to the next, we're like the Ancient Ones following the magnetic waters of life and the energetic ley lines of the earth from one sacred site to the next. Each moment, each site, is an opportunity to raise consciousness, invite in healing, and open to the Mystery within and all around us.

There are no rules or rush when it comes to living and visioning with the flow along the ley lines of love. Go with your heart's pulse and trust in the wisdom of your being.

· RITUAL ·
Following Love's Ley Lines

Your heart is the center of the magnetic field all around you and part of the greater field of the Universe. This field is a matrix of possibilities, all created according to your mental, emotional, and physical state in the present moment. Each cultivated thought and conscious emotion draws you through the field toward the next spectrum of possibilities.

Thoughts are *electric*; emotions, *magnetic*. When you want to create an expansive and abundant vision for your purpose, it's your positively charged thoughts that put you on an aligned wavelength and your heartfelt emotions that magnetize what you desire into your life. Every positive thought has a healing, uplifting impact on your body/form, energy/spirit, heart/emotions, and mind/presence. At this time of global awakening, every positive thought, every peaceful feeling, every high-vibrational emotion is impacting the entire consciousness of humanity. Here are some ways to keep in tune with a positive, uplifting outlook without overlooking the denser emotions or negative thoughts that require your healing attention.

- Start each day with a unique and specific affirmation that states what you're ready to receive. Match a positive emotion to the affirmation—genuinely connect to the feeling that comes with it—and smile bravely, boldly, knowingly. Once this affirmation has been declared, follow the ley lines throughout your day.

- Ask for gifts from the Universe and be sure to look out for offerings that perhaps aren't wrapped in a bow, such as a smile from a stranger or a new flower blooming in your garden. Pause to open your heart and receive the gift.

- Ask for healing and look for what life shows you when you're ready to heal. Welcome new healing modalities that come into your realm and pay attention to healers' names that arise in conversations with friends.

- If you require assistance with the vision you're creating for your purposeful life, ask the Universe to show you the essential aspects of your new vision. If you're feeling stuck, keep moving physically and mentally through your day with graceful fluidity, pausing to notice the visions that come your way—in dreams, magazines, social media, books, and the places you visit. Keep dancing with all of life as the vision braids itself in your hands and heart.

- Choose a simple temple, a sacred space in your home, or a favorite spot in nature that reminds you of the important and purposeful ley line you're on. Set an intention for the temple to be healing; let it soothe and surrender dense emotions while you spend precious time there meditating on love.

As you open your magnetic heart center to the bounty all around you, the way you naturally flow over ley lines of radiant purpose will become clearer and more abundant.

Revering the Void and Rainbows of Promise

As you continue traveling through life, you will inevitably come across periods of emptiness. During these times, you may feel like all creativity has been drained from you and you have nothing to give or share. Don't fear these moments; embrace them. For they are as important as the exuberant and creative days to come.

· Journey ·
Going Deep into the Storm

Picture yourself on a rainy morning as your beloved sleeps deeply. You're taking a quiet walk through a subtle ravine. Moss blankets each rock, ferns sweep their grace along the sloped earth, palms gather in luscious clusters, and a creek meanders, collecting pace leisurely as rain drenches the earth.

The heavier the rain, the deeper you go into the ravine, until you find a large, curved rock to shelter under. In the dampness and shade, you release your baggage, setting your load and limbs down in total surrender. You soak up the heaviness of the thick clouds and constant showers. After a little while of ignoring your inner state, you tune in to see what the elements are mirroring within you. Tears flow from the corners of your eyes; wordless, endless saltwater streams through your vision, cleansing and clearing, healing and releasing. As the tears slow down, you take a deep breath and relax. The rain falls harder, leaving you no choice but to rest in the rocky cavern until the storm has passed.

As the storm becomes louder, your thoughts come howling to life. The dark clouds usher in space for a harsh voice that arises from within. Lashings of criticism, judgment, and disapproval flood your heart. In the darkest reaches of your mind, there seems to be nowhere to hide.

For a timeless stretch, this continues, thought against thought, until you surrender the ego's games and let the sharp fragments go in three raucously loud breaths. Leaning on the rocks for solace, you feel the pull of earth holding you close, the smoothness of each rock soothing your inner storm. Feeling like you've softened your edges, you come back to presence with clarity and watch the rest of the storm in peace.

Throughout the day, thunder and lightning play out in the basin in front of you; you feel the energy of the elements unleashing their power in perfect harmony with each other. There's no such thing as *too big* in nature, and your emotional state is no different. Your heart settles into a harmonious state; whatever was hidden has come to light in the darkness of this perfect day.

Eventually the storm calms and the sun streams out, illuminating each suspended raindrop on trees and plants, flowers and rocks, and your tear-stained cheeks. You rejoice at the virtuousness of a personal cleanse reflected in the composition of nature. Your inner elements have returned to a higher state; your mind has surrendered confusion and attachment, and your body feels lighter.

Stepping out of the valley and onto a more level path, you see a rainbow light up the east as the sun sets in the west. With appreciation, you walk home.

SITTING CONSCIOUSLY IN THE VOID

Within all of us is a void: an endless space of darkness. This cavern cannot be known or mapped; its contents are invisible to the human self. This is the limitless birthplace of all creativity, an energetic womb.

It feels infinitely empty ... *it's supposed to.*

For many, the emptiness, the unknown, the limitlessness is too much because the mind cannot grasp what is within this space. For others, the exact same characteristics are what make the void mysterious, exciting, and approachable. How we connect with our void is important along the route of purpose. If we cannot bear to be alone, we may never get quiet enough to hear the subtleties of our heart's song. If we cannot embrace endings, we will never know the taste of the sweetest beginnings. If we cannot fathom a concept or idea without logic, we many never know how powerful our intuitive dreaming and visioning are.

"When we show up to make art, we need to first get still enough to hear what wants to be expressed through us, and then we need to step out of the way and let it," writes Mirabai Starr in her wonderfully crafted book *Wild Mercy*. She goes on to write, "We must be willing to abide in a space of not knowing before we can settle into knowing. Such a space is sacred."[6]

Sitting consciously in the void is a sacred act.

"Art" is anything creative, and creativity comes always from the heart. When you listen to the bold and brave, sweet and subtle, artistic wishes of your heart, you must first step into the void of your being for a moment to let the mystery speak.

---

6. Mirabai Starr, *Wild Mercy: Living the Fierce and Tender Wisdom of the Women Mystics* (Boulder, CO: Sounds True, 2019), 159.

Sometimes the elements within us conspire to bring us closer to the void, the inner well of darkness where there is nothing to fear and everything to heal. If we resist and run, we will never feel complete, never know the grand wholeness of our being. If we accept and dive in, we must face whatever arises.

Consciousness is light. When you become aware of something about yourself that you previously didn't know, you're shining the light of consciousness into the shadow of unconsciousness. There doesn't need to be a reaction or a process of fixing what you see or understand; sacred consciousness is enough. See it, love it, and let it move through you to heal you.

You can come to know your shadow on a deeper level when you become conscious of your past, curious about your beliefs, and responsible for your reactions. Your shadow is the repressed, suppressed, forgotten, dismissed, unloved, and unwanted parts of you. If your parents, caregivers, teachers, friends, peers, or partners did not like some aspect of you, and made it clear to you what was unacceptable, then you may have hidden it away to please or appease them.

When you take time to sit *consciously in the void* of your being, you will often find your inner child or younger self showing you an aspect of them you rejected in order to feel more accepted by others. This aspect of you has so much to tell you and only wants to be loved and accepted. Through patience and understanding, you can welcome it back into your being and feel more whole. You may find that this part of you leads to a wonderfully significant development in your purpose.

The void is the black hole of your being, the beginning and the end of the Universe within. There is no inspired creation without this empty space; it's from here we create all visions worthy of our attention. In the nothingness within, found in quiet stillness, we enter the realm of all that is. This is where the clearest vision for your purpose is waiting to be birthed.

As a child is seeded by its father, grown by its mother, and birthed from the womb, so, too, all of creation is seeded by the divine masculine energy of light/consciousness (a bright spark, an idea), grown by the divine feminine energy of love/creation (nurturing care), and birthed from the darkness, the womb of life.

The greatest, most creative ideas of my life have come from moments of complete surrender to nothingness. When I genuinely give up what I know, what I want, and all expectations, I'm given a miracle. First the storm rages—chaos often precedes creation—and cleanses my attachments, then the calm comes, and serenity wraps me in her comforting blanket of clouds, and finally the rainbow of creation lights up my whole being.

In the catastrophic storm that swept through Byron Bay in early 2022, flooding this sacred land we live on and changing everyone's lives without exception, my purpose became ravenously clear. I craved women's sacred circles in my home, I wanted to host more loving and healing retreats, I envisioned a shift in my online community, and I discovered a deeper way of channeling Spirit as I worked with clients. For months after the flood, I was unable to create anything; I didn't have a car, my internet was unstable, the roads to my home were a weathered mess, and my health needed extensive care. In this sacred pause, I trusted, waited, and held these visions close to my heart. In due course, it all unfolded in divinely perfect timing. It is still unfolding, forever. Life continues to surprise me with the profound simplicity and beauty of my purpose since being cleansed and healed by the most intense ordeal of my life.

Create a vision that feels like you're looking at a full sky of vibrant double rainbows. Whenever you need to begin again, wash the slate clean, plant a new seed of intention, go into stillness for as long as you need, and allow the vision to be rebirthed under skies of brilliance and wonder.

Storms will come when we least expect them, but always when we're energetically in need of a fresh start. Your rainbows won't look like anyone else's; they will be made of the colors of your luminous light and feel like medicine and salt water.

· RITUAL ·
Wild Inner Child Connection

Inner child connection is powerful healing work. I have a picture of myself as a child on my altar; I look at her sweet face often. I found an image of the happiest version of me to remind myself of how wonderful my childhood was. I experienced many kinds of traumas throughout my younger years, but I've forgiven all involved and feel incredibly at peace.

If you have a photo of yourself as a child, hold it for this ritual. If not, simply imagine a happy, smiling moment when you were a child. Try the following process without getting stuck in an old narrative that paints you as a victim. Approach these steps with forgiveness, acceptance, and peace.

1. Sit where you won't be disturbed. Set an intention to meet with your inner child in a way that is comfortable, liberating, compassionate, and loving. Play gentle music through headphones if that helps you feel calm and focused.

2. Imagine you as a child sitting in front of the current you. Open your heart to your younger self and ask what they would like to share with you. Be patient; trust what you hear, see, or know. Take your time

with this step and be present to their innocence that still lives within you.

3. Ask them what they think about your life purpose, your ancient gifts, and your intuitive talents. Consider how this insight can be helpful to you on your path.

4. Now take time to share a few loving thoughts with your inner child. Tell them all you wanted to hear as a child, but no one ever told you, or you didn't hear it enough. Tell them how wonderful it is to be you, living this wild life. Tell them whatever pours from your heart that helps them feel safely held, deeply loved, and truly seen.

5. When you feel complete, acknowledge them with love and compassion and imagine hugging them until they melt into you.

Sit with this feeling for as long as you need to; allow love to move through you. Give thanks for your childhood and all the blessings that are in your current life because of it.

SURRENDER TO THE GUIDANCE OF THE WIND

When life gets loud, surrender to it. Resisting or dismissing the commotion within or around you will cause a repressive storm to brew and erupt in the future. Instead, *surrender*.

· JOURNEY ·
Revering the Infinite Lifeforce

Imagine you are walking for some time with a veritable rainbow cloaked around you. Having felt the cleanse of rain, you're ready to welcome a period of peace. Everyone in your community has been through some form of purification or cleansing, and you're enjoying the process of coming together with a harmonious group of high-vibrational beings.

Just as you hang your clothes out to dry and clean up your tent, ready to nurture yourself and embrace new connections, a breeze stirs up anything not tied down. Everyone packs away anything that's unstable, with much laughter between you all. Soon the wind picks up enough to make cooking dinner difficult, with dirt and leaves flying onto food and cutlery strewn all around. You make it to bed early only to lie awake for hours, wondering if your tent will stay secure. And in the morning, you find everyone in a similarly overtired flux.

For the next few days, the unyielding wind courses through your community, making conversations arduous, music impossible, and leisure laborious. Communal fires aren't safe, clothes become dirty as they dry, and everyday moments of joy and wonder disappear.

One evening, alone in your tent, you release your frustration in a long and deep *ommm*. Your expression becomes lost in the outrageous wind, so you hum your *ommm* again—this time, a little louder. After three grounding, healing *ommms*, you feel the peace you've been craving for days. This state of repose feels like you are the eye of the storm, and nothing is agitating you in this precious moment. You smile, and your body ripples with bliss. With your resistance gone, you lie down and sleep peacefully.

In the morning, the bright sun wakes you. You step out of the tent to the sound of birds and not even a hint of a breeze—a welcome sensation. Others wake from their sleep to join you in the morning sunshine; eyes sparkling, they take a deep breath to drink in the divine stillness of a calm morning.

You feel like you conquered the storm within you once more. This initiation from the elements has given you a renewed connection to your inner strength, and you stand taller because of it. Soon, someone starts a fire to take the chill out of the air, and you all gather around it to share stories, songs, and breakfast, hearts overflowing with gratitude.

THE EVOLUTION OF PURPOSE

There are two concepts that make me extremely uncomfortable: wind and change. The term *winds of change* sends a mildly anxious chill up my spine.

My heart isn't afraid of change. It knows deep down how it can be a good (sometimes extremely good) process, but all too often my ego resists change when I'm not the one making it happen. I can see how obviously that shows my issues around control. (I'm working on it.)

Wind rattles me. I can't seem to settle my mind on a windy day or sleep deeply on a blustery night. I've been told it's because I'm an air sign. Perhaps as a Gemini this is ultimately my fate *and* lesson: to surrender to the gale, to make peace with change, and to find stability within, no matter what the elements or my life's circumstances are up to.

To evolve along the *evolution of purpose*, we need to be mindfully attuned to the truth within us and honor that each day, even—and especially—if that means changing our opinions, connections, and situations. As humans, we have the ability to learn, to change our mind, and to pivot our lives. If we are aware of the limitations placed on us by our ego, we can dissolve them through the faculty of consciousness. We can gently witness them and, through compassion, allow them to step aside.

Although I hesitate to make big changes, I've learned how great change can be, from changing my mind to changing my address. I attach less pride to each belief, all parts of my identity, every possession, and all personal opinions so that when the need to pivot comes, it's done with as little resistance and as much grace as possible.

As I flow through projects, creations, and jobs, I've learned to be in sync with the wind. The only way I've found to be happy throughout my career is to trust that every step is somehow perfect, that whatever the wind sweeps from my hands—such as job opportunities and creative collaborations—wasn't meant for me at the time. I have such deep, deep trust in my path that I'm rarely disappointed, and I'm learning to make friends with the wind and dance her unpredictable dance with her.

There's a Higher Power that is always looking out for your needs, like the spirit of the wind who has your best interests at heart. Coursing through life with infinite trust, like a breeze blowing through a valley, means not holding on to the vision that you've created too tightly. You've got to let the wind mess with it a little. And here's the beauty of having a vision: Without words, it becomes more than an identity, a possession, or a goal. It becomes an outward, living expression of the essence of you. These expressions already live within you. By creating a vision, you allow space for the expressions to manifest in and around your life.

Let's say your vision is one of sitting in a circle with other like-hearted people. Holding that vision will draw you into sacred circle work, but as the winds blow through your life, the vision may not manifest in the way you think it will. If you're able to trust the vision but hold the details gently, the wind will shape your circumstances to reflect the direction of your Soul's work.

There is so much power in creating and holding a vision within the chambers of your heart, but if it has too many thoughts, predictions, limitations, or presumptions, it won't be adaptable to the elements of life.

Create your vision with all the visual detail you desire. Call in all the aspects that make up your most joyful, abundant, and incomparable purpose. Fill your journal and your home with images of the wildhearted work you're stepping into. Call it a five- or ten-year plan and write down how much money you'd like to make. Just don't forget to notice when life begins to reflect the visions of your heart. Don't neglect to give thanks to the Universe for meeting you where you're at with a wealth of treasures. And when the wind comes, don't resist the mighty sway. Stand firm and fluid in the tempest, reconnect to your ancient core, and let the debris be swept onward, clearing space for a new way to live on *the evolution of your purpose.*

· RITUAL ·
Anchoring into Self Meditation

During windy times of turbulence, uncertainty, or upheaval, there's a simple meditation that helps me feel grounded and held. Be in nature if you can; otherwise, imagine you are. Sit or stand with feet flat on the ground or earth. Here's how I flow through it.

1. Set an intention. Call on your Soul's light to fill and surround your energetic field. State your intention and how you would like to feel by the end of this meditation, such as grounded, strong, held, safe, or unperturbed.

2. Close your eyes and breathe into your nose to fill your belly; let it soften completely. Breathe out of

your mouth. As you slowly exhale, let go of tension, anxiety, and fear. Repeat three times. Come back to breathing naturally; let your lifeforce flow with ease.

3. Feel the energy that pulses within the soles of your feet. Each sole has its own chakra, which creates an energetic portal from your body into the earth. Imagine the light from your heart glowing stronger, then flowing down your legs, through the chakras of your feet, into the earth, and all the way to the planet's core. Now imagine your energy being infused by the grounding, healing, and nurturing energy of Mother Earth. Visualize your energy spreading all the way through the earth. Stay with that feeling as long as you need, then bring this earthly energy up through your roots, activating the chakras on your feet.

4. Let this grounded energy wash all the way through your system from your feet to your hips, belly, and heart, down your arms to your fingertips, up your neck and head to your crown chakra and beyond, and all through your auric field. Feel you and Mother Earth as one. Feel your bright light in Her, and Her grounding love within you.

5. When you feel complete, give thanks and stretch your body.

THE SPIRAL OF GROWTH AND PURPOSE

Just when you think you've reached a higher state of being, you realize there is more to learn, heal, or forgive from your past. It's easy to see this in the light of failure and become frustrated at your lack of progress, but if you could see your journey from a greater perspective, you'd see the sacred spiral of your life unraveling in perfect timing.

· JOURNEY ·

Labyrinths and Awakening

Take a moment to picture your beloved, or simply feel what it might be like to hold the hand of a loved one as you look for a new landscape of flourishing gardens to live on. You're calling in a deeper state of harmony within yourself, between you and your partner, on a patch of land under the stars. You know you will be guided to a place that is promising for you both to learn and grow.

As you walk with your love, a conversation on lifelong dreams turns into a discussion about star families, spirit animals, herbal wisdom, and early memories. You have so much to learn from and share with your beloved that you wander happily, feet connected by a mutual rhythm, hearts in tune with a sense of adventure, and minds in engaging conversation.

After a while, you notice familiar footprints on the ground a short distance away, and you realize you've been hiking around in a circle, though not quite a perfect circle—more like the beginning of a spiral. You pause to take in the path you've traversed so far, to consider that after all the effort you put into that stretch, you're standing so close to where you started out this morning. To your logical mind, this means you've made no real, practical ground. There's a voice in your head that's frustrated at what seems like a waste of time, but you're in such a heightened state of loving connection that you ignore your irked ego and instead wonder at the mysterious and unknown perfection along your path.

With a collective smile, you pause for lunch. For the rest of the afternoon, you intentionally complete the shape of the spiral until you come to the center just before dark. Something within you feels complete, like an indiscernible inward process has been achieved. The two of you set up camp for the night and gather stones to create a circle for a firepit. The day has felt so valuable, so divinely guided, and together you sleep deeply by the fire.

In the morning, you wake under golden hues of the morning sun to discover that your love has created a labyrinth within the center of the spiral with the abundance of rocks warm from the overnight flames.

Still connected to tranquil dream states and guided by a force without words, you set a simple intention and walk slowly along the arches and around the bends. Your feet have moved like this in many lifetimes; this path is new today, and yet familiar. Another unraveling occurs, this time with tears and sighs. You resist conscious reasoning and open to the inner flow of your heart, the way it directs the body without words—with a wisdom from beyond—to a place of restoration.

Afterward, you sit in the shade, blissfully eating a late breakfast, feeling as though you've untangled a thousand inner knots. As your love moves through the labyrinth, you notice the warm hues of light rising in the sky and appreciate that the sun makes a similar curve overhead as the rocks do on the ground. As your love's legs move back and forth, the rays shine on each crescent of rocks. You close your eyes halfway and feel into the energetic interplay of the earth, rocks, sun, and stars. You notice a few snails with their spiral shells slinking past you onto a fern that's all curled up. You see this symbol of awakening everywhere. There's a magic here that's consciously out of reach and yet a natural part of your ancient Soul's knowing.

Within this sun-blessed magic, you rest.

SYNCING INNER AND OUTER GALAXIES

Your purpose can only come from the depths of *your* heart, yet it comes to life, becomes tangible, and makes a difference the moment it touches the heart of *another*.

Taking time to journey with your inner yearnings while also making space to connect with others—to cocreate, collaborate, and open to the fusion of purposeful energy—is the balance we all need to strive for on this wildhearted adventure of our lifetime.

Other people will test you, challenge you, and belittle you. This is the easiest way to discover your shadowed insecurities, to feel into what needs healing, even if the words and actions of another come from their own insecurities and unhealed aspects. Other people will also lift you up, celebrate you, inspire you, and alchemize your medicine with theirs. This is how you know you've found a Soul brother or sister, one who aligns with the vibration of your light. Like walking a spiral arm-in-arm with a friend, Soul family will make the journey less challenging and support you in your discoveries.

During time with partners, lovers, friends, community, family, children, and other companions, you may discover that opportunities to sit still are rare. You may feel like you've got to keep learning, trying, evolving, surrendering, seeking, healing, failing, and praying. But only you know what you need in any given moment. This is your journey.

The Universe will always send us the people we need—the Soul family, the beloved ones—right when we need them. Know when you need time to be alone and take these opportunities without guilt, with full reverence for your spirit. Like walking a labyrinth in peace, some things in life are meant to be experienced on your own. Likewise, it's important to step out of your quiet shell and connect with others when the silence is ever pervading.

You become consciously spiritual the moment you remember you are a Soul on a human journey and there is a Higher Power that wants you to have the most incredible life imaginable. Once this awareness lands in your being, it will never leave you. You will always remember who you really are—glistening light present for a while in an earthly body.

The spiral has long been a symbol for the spiritual journey throughout history. It shows us that we keep circling back to touch on what we've already learned to discover deeper truths, new awareness, and higher learning from other people and situations. We never go backward; it's impossible. The spiral continuously grows as we become more conscious, more aware of life and the expansion inherent in it.

The spiral has been my favorite symbol to draw ever since I was little. Each book, journal, and diary I own has spirals drawn in it. With each spiral, I feel tension unwinding and releasing. I feel a similar ease simply by looking at a series of spirals. There's no right or perfect way to draw or live a spiraled life. It's the natural force from within us, from within all of nature.

Spirals are all around us: our galaxy is one, many plants and shells grow in that way, and water and energy often flow like spiral vortexes. The spiritual life is a spiral of enlightenment. The evolution of our life is like a spiral; as we move toward the center, we surrender the ego and come closer home to Source.

The vision for your journey can be as simple as a spiral or as complex as a labyrinth. Each has its own concealed and felt magic. Along your purpose, however it looks, it's helpful to touch on symbols and signs, geometry and formations, ripples and dunes in the natural world of your wild being. Allow these to activate a deeper awareness of the path you walk.

Life is a never-ending spiral of raising consciousness and deepening awareness. There is no real destination. We're all *syncing inner and outer galaxies.*

· RITUAL ·
Symbolic Journeys in Nature

Creating your own symbolic journey in nature is incredibly rewarding, healing, and playful. It's valuable when you're in need of closure on a project or your business is pivoting into a new chapter. Here are some ideas to bring this ritual into your life.

- Draw a spiral on a large area of sand or dirt. Make the paths wide enough to easily walk through without disturbing the lines or lay a thick vine or rope on top of the etched spiral. Set an intention for this journey and allow it to unfold organically. During your spiral walk, you may discover what you're ready to let go of or catch a glimpse of where you are heading. Allow the visions and messages to come as they may.

- Use rocks to create a labyrinth. Find basic or intricate layouts online and use stones to align with the curves of the sun's arch during the day. Walk the labyrinth by setting an intention, then moving through the maze to the center, pausing to receive answers, pray, or share your gratitude, then walk back the way you came all the way to the start. Never leave a labyrinth without walking all the way in and out, otherwise you break the intention.

- Let yourself draw or doodle on a blank piece of paper without letting your thoughts get in the way. Explore symbology intuitively through the drawings you create.

· PRACTICE ·

Higher Vision Soul Prompts

As we wrap up the first part of this book together, I want to share a handful of creative journal prompts that will help you gain a clearer vision of what you've created so far on your wildhearted journey and where your heart wants to go next.

Your Soul has begun to stir with creative ideas and ancient longings. The stories, symbols, elements, metaphors, and images in this part are the keys for unlocking what has been dormant or out of reach so far in your life. With the following questions, I'd encourage you to allow your heart to answer in any way it desires, perhaps through words, symbols, or images. Express yourself in any way that feels good. There's no need to go into too much detail as that's what we're digging into in the next section: a blissfully elaborate design for your purpose that you can come back to—and redesign when necessary—all over again.

- How does your heart feel at the thought of living on purpose in the creative chaos of your wild nature? What experiences do you love in nature, and how do these show up in your purpose?

- What visions have appeared so far on your journey through these pages? How are they weaving themselves together and what can you sense is taking shape?

- What excites you about following the ley lines of love? Are you able to fully trust in this deeper form of guidance? Can you feel your intuition pulling you onward?

- How would you describe your Soul's unique medicine? What does it look, sound, and feel like? How are you noticing and honoring it?

- Can you see how radiant and successful you are already? Can you sink into this abundant inner wealth and acknowledge all that you have created in your life?

- What storms have you encountered recently and how are you stronger for them? Can you allow the storms to pass without getting caught up in them? Can you anchor yourself into your own sovereign and energetic roots when the wind blows? Are you noticing the rainbows, the calmness, the purification afterward?

- What is the greatest, highest, most abundant vision you have for your life? Draw this or write it out in detail. Don't hold back; you are a boundless being capable of *anything*.

Part Two
GROW YOUR DESIGN

Your purpose is inimitably yours. If it is authenticity, abundance, service, and satisfaction you're seeking, you won't find it along an established process created by another. The only thing you'll find on the paved, mapped roads is other peoples' purpose. And while that might be entertaining and inspiring, it's *not your purpose*.

In order to design your *own* process, you'll need to use the vision you created in the first part and call in the aspects of your blueprint until what unfolds in front of you feels completely and truly yours. This section is the important step of designing a grounded and powerful yet flexible and resilient process that blooms from your Soul. After all, the term *on purpose* was written as far back as the sixteenth century to mean "by design, intentionally."

Along the veracious course of your heart, there cannot be a map. And if long-term goals are part of your design, allow plenty of intuitive fluidity so you're still able to follow the light beams of your Soul.

Come with me into the wild where we'll tap into a process that's just right for you.

Chapter 4

ALCHEMIZE THE CLUTTER

"Every life is an unprecedented experiment. This life is mine alone.
So I have stopped asking people for directions to
places they've never been.
There is no map. We are all pioneers."[7]
—GLENNON DOYLE

The path you take is the path you create if you want to live an authentic purpose. There will always be other people around you to give you advice, tell you what to do, how to do it, and when to stop. From within you there will be misaligned distractions, insecure procrastination, and unexpected conclusions. And underneath it all will be your calmly determined Soul, knowing, trusting, attuning, and nudging you onward.

This chapter is about taking your vision and laying it out before you—not so much as a formula to predict or persuade your future, but as an expression of your inner compass that calls you onto the next passage. Before you take that step, you'll need to let go of everything heavy or misaligned that's weighing you down and capture the beauty of what you'll find in the lightness that ensues.

---

7.   Glennon Doyle, *Untamed* (New York: The Dial Press, 2020), 60.

BURN THE MAP THEY GAVE YOU

Everyone wants you to have their map. They found a route that took them where they wanted to go, and they just *know* it will work for you. Except it won't. Because it can't. Only you and the wild know where you're going.

· JOURNEY ·
The Great Mystery Embodied

Take a moment to imagine a peach-hued sunrise, blessing you on the beginning of the next phase of your journey. You pause long enough to build a small fire; it warms you on this refreshing early morning. In your dreams last night, you were shown symbolically that you are carrying with you the desires of people in your past. After you pack your belongings and sit by the fire, you're drawn to find a piece of paper from your bag and write on it what you saw in your dream.

As you write this down in detail, you realize unquestionably that every map ever made for you is pulling you away from your true north.

When you are complete, you toss this collection of maps, drawings, and memories into the flames. You watch until it all burns to ash, then laugh gratefully as a rain cloud moves over the firepit and showers over the ashes. Inhaling deeply, you feel as clear as the rain's refreshing scent, all external direction falling away and leaving you with a sense of peaceful anticipation.

You look around the clearing you're in. You can discern where you came from, but with endless possibilities around you, it's not obvious where to go next. In the spaciousness of your newfound freedom, you feel wondrously deluged with possibilities. Without a map, the unknown wraps itself around you and beckons you.

Lingering in this state, you close your eyes and place your hands on your heart. Asking your innermost guide where you're headed, you feel the spirit of the morning fire calming your mind, strengthening your body, and awakening your Soul.

The words of the fire spirit are gentle and precise:

Your unattached, untamed Soul knows the way according to the compass set by your heart. Listen deeply.

Love and truth are the directions and the only destinations worth pursuing, but they are not on any map. Do not rush this process, precious one.

Pursue it gently, fearlessly, and in faith that the great mystery is the deepest essence of you. Go now.

When you open your eyes, you give thanks to the fire for its wisdom and medicine. The moment you feel ready to move, you hear the laughter of a flock of birds and know that this boisterous call of bliss from the horizon is yours to follow until joy moves you in another direction. Your love comes to join you after their morning of foraging for food.

As you marvel in awe at the process of alchemy that swept through you from the dream to the fire, you wander off without expectation as to where you're going or how you'll get there. Being able to hear your heart breathe is all the direction you need.

SURRENDERING DEPENDENCY

At the beginning of every new journey, a map is sought. Whether the map lies within the neuropathways of your mind or beyond you as colored lines on paper, it provides a deep sigh of comfort. It shows you exactly where you are and makes it clear that the steps you need to take have already been decided. With a map, all you have to do is follow the paved paths around mountains and beside lakes, jump on the chalked hopscotch of your career and the stepping-stones of each relationship, and you'll arrive wherever you're meant to go.

The wildhearted journey is different. This journey is taking you to a moveable destination of loving authenticity and honest service, so there's no external latitude or longitude to fix your sights on. There's nowhere you're *meant* to be. The coordinates are heartfelt and change according to the necessary whims of your Soul. It's not possible to drop a pin onto the ever-evolving, transforming journey sought after by the deepest desires of your timeless, ancient being.

Your heart on this journey of discovery declares that all maps are fraudulent because they come from an external source. No one can possibly know the path of your wild heart or where you're destined to go. People can show you where they've been, they can tell you where they're going, but they cannot begin to fathom what route is the most advantageous or appropriate for you.

In your hands you hold countless maps handed to you from others in your past. Some were sincere and others deceitful. There are those who gave you advice based on what had worked brilliantly for them or what they saw as possible for you. Perhaps this was well-meaning and kind, intended to help or point you in a particularly positive direction. However, *all* maps are now no longer required. There's real power in *surrendering dependency*.

As a mentor, I love sharing possibilities with clients based on what I can intuitively see for them. My opinions may come from my psychic senses and intuitive experience, my university degree and mentor training, but they're still just an opinion. The word *opinion* comes from the Latin words *visium* meaning "view" and *videre* meaning "to see." My advice or opinion is only what *I see* for each client, which can be remarkably empowering, but I don't believe it should ever be followed perfectly or without patient reflection.

All advice must be passed through the intuitive knowing of your heart center before it can land as a possibility in your being. Energetically there must be a match; when there is, this is called alignment. This feels like expansiveness and sunshine. When an idea is aligned with your energy, it doesn't mean you must do what you've been told to do; it simply means it's a feasible and fertile idea.

If your life is being played out according to a bundle of maps that have been handed to you by people from your past, such as caregivers, parents, siblings, teachers, mentors, peers, books, and the media, then it's not your most authentic life. Authenticity will deliver the highest state of bliss, peace, and fulfillment along your path. It calls you to be as genuine, honest, original, and heartfelt as possible in all you do and *surrender dependency* to others.

It's not easy to live in the unknown. Uncertainty enrages and exasperates people. We are conditioned to seek certainty from outside of us: in a job, an employer, a regular salary, a routine, a partner, a wedding ring, a promise, material possessions, the government, organizations, and health practitioners. But if we're being honest with ourselves, none of this gives us any real sense of security, because only change is certain. Knowing that nothing on earth is certain means we can empower ourselves with our connection to our spirit. Our anchor must be within us, for the only certainty is our infinite invisible Soul. We are born to live an unpredictable life; if we knew how it would play out, we wouldn't learn the lessons we need to on a Soul level or be surprised by the variety and spontaneity of life.

Nature is our greatest teacher; our Soul, our wisest guide. As we do away with the maps and look around us, past our possessions and identity, past the guidelines and rules, there is always only nature. As we surrender control and look within us, beyond our expectations and attachments, beyond beliefs and limitations, there is our infinite nature, our Soul.

Spending time in nature helps the vision of your purpose find its fullest expression. As you feel your way through nature with your senses, your mind softens, needs for specific outcomes fade, scripts and prescriptions melt away, and you open your heart to the present moment. It's through nothingness that you'll find *everything* you need. The unfathomable emptiness within you is all you can ever really be sure of. It's your connection to Source, God and Goddess, Divine Love—to all you have ever been, all you will ever be, and all you are capable of right now.

Connecting rapturously to the invisible threads of light empowers you to regularly dive into the mystical abyss, the unknown field. Finding familiarity in this space through meditation and nature connection not only gives you a sense of inner ease, but it strengthens you every day as you walk among loud messages, angry people, fearful narratives, and hectic energy. We are living through the end of the dark ages and the beginning of the Age of Light. This new age means the death of fear, separation, false power, media coercion, suppressing systems, and anything that goes against the grain of love. It's a tumultuous time to be alive.

It's also the most incredible time to be here—to design together a New Earth, a greater purpose for all, individually and as One. Old maps in your life that are heavy, misaligned, or outdated can be thrown into the fire and alchemized into something much greater. You have the power to transmute and transform the old ways and programs into a fresh, new approach in communion with Mother Nature.

Creating a design that involves a deeper connection to the depths of love within will give you a clearer sense of direction along the path of your purpose than anything else. Looking to nature for your answers as you design and redesign your purpose is as important as it is nurturing, helpful, and heartening.

You don't need a map; you need to trust the infinite, wordless language of love streaming from your heart each day.

· RITUAL ·
Violet Flame Alchemy of Purpose

We touched on violet flame alchemy earlier in the book, and now I want to take you through a more in-depth ritual for you to use in any area of your life that needs refreshing.

The violet flame has been an important part of healing on my spiritual path. I've found that, as with any ritual, the more attention I pay to what I'm doing and the more I experience it with all my inner senses, the more powerful the effect. Here's how I call on transmutation in my life with the violet flame.

1. Begin by finding a space where you won't be disturbed. Sit upright and take a few deep breaths in through your nose and out of your mouth.

2. When you feel relaxed, imagine what negativity or unease you'd like to raise the vibration of. It could be your overall purpose, your beliefs about self-worth, your current job, or a virtual bunch of old maps that you're ready to let go of. See clearly with your mind's eye what it is you're ready to surrender to a higher form.

3. Call on the violet flame. Ask it to surround you and your vision with the violet flame. Notice cool purple flames all around you and the maps, ideas, people, places, and situations you're tending to.

4. Ask the violet flame now to transmute all low, dense, and negative energies into higher ones. You don't need to know what these are transmuting into; just spend some time holding the violet flame in this place until you notice a shift. The shift may be a shiver in your body, a knowing in your heart, a deeper-than-normal breath, or something else that alerts you to the alchemy having taken place.

5. Once the vibration of your vision has been raised, you can ask questions of your Soul, or you may receive a knowing right away what the higher outcome is. Trust that a change has taken place and that you're now in a place of divine love, expansive healing, and true power. Take out your notebook if anything comes to you that you want to note down.

6. Give thanks for the violet flame.

You can use this alchemical process for strained relationships, imbalanced health, feeling lost, stuck energy, dense emotions, or unfulfilled dreams. I encounter miracle after miracle with this process, and I trust you will, too.

The more time you spend in nature, the more you'll feel how Her energy naturally transmutes your energy from low to high, from fear to love, from forced to graceful. As you let go of these outdated ways of being, you'll find it so much easier to design all that is yearning to be created by the architect within. During this process of intimate surrender, you'll stop grasping for anything outside of yourself. Your design will come from a deeper place, as though it's etched in light within the essence of your being.

You're Already Doing It

Woven within all that you are already being and doing are the threads of the fabric for the next part of your purpose. All that you love, all that you're healing, all that calls to you, is entwining together for a reason. Whatever you're craving for the future already exists within you now.

· Journey ·
Parcels of Gratitude

Imagine you are in a state of deep rest, and within this rest you experience a dream where you sit for a long time with a mountain of great stature, soaking up the healing, perspective, and strength emitted from this ancient being. In your lucid dream you soar with eagles, dance on rain clouds, and merge with a golden sunrise. When you wake from your slumber, you're eager to find this mountain as the visions in your sleep often anticipate the day ahead.

After breakfast and yoga, you walk toward this unseen summit, following nature's signs and symbols. Every step is in faith, but you feel empty-handed. This sacred journey promises to saturate you with loving abundance, and you would like to be prepared with a gift.

Resting in a field with your lunch, contemplating what to give the mountain, you remember the natural creations you crafted as a kid. Fanned bundles of dried eucalyptus leaves for tossing on the fire, chains of daisies, parcels of seeds wrapped in large rubbery leaves, clay dishes imprinted with textural bark, bouquets of unruly feathers, impossibly balanced rock piles, and lavender wands.

Your senses are heightened, more perceptive of the offerings all around you as you walk through the grass collecting treasures from the earth's floor. Grass becomes swiftly woven into a shallow basket, which is filled with fallen flowers and seeds. Sap glues feathers to the center of your traveling altar, and colorful pebbles bring the masterpiece together. You're deeply spellbound by this craft, which floods you with memories of holidays in the forest, and you miss the mountain's introduction in the distance. When you finally look up, it takes your breath away. Your feet hurry along, eager to be closer to this tremendous being. Your energy and smile expand wider as you draw closer.

At the first sight of a large, smooth gray rock, you fall to your knees in elation, placing your precious gift in the grass that grows through a crack in the rock. The simple act of presenting this gift fills you with the sweetest of emotions; you created it from the joy of your inner child and are elated to be connected to your long-lost talents. With joyful tears streaming down your cheeks, you kiss the rock and ask for permission to climb halfway, as high as the tallest tree. Feeling your heartspace lighten, you know you are welcome here in this safe place of transformation. With a humble bow of thanks, a blessing given, and a prayer for protection shared, you begin.

IGNITING THE SPARK ALREADY WITHIN

We all have so much goodness and radiance to offer. From our ancient gifts to our lifelong talents, soul-deep medicine, and healing presence, we are already full of abundant offerings. Life isn't all about acquiring brilliance, skill, and technique, although all of that inevitably adds to your credibility and character; it's about discovering what's already in you, designing ways to share that freely, and allowing the Universe to express its gratitude in return.

As I connect with my mentoring clients who are searching for the best career path, I find myself tuning in to gifts they are already sharing with others—that perhaps they are overlooking—and what they did for pleasure and joy as a child that was swept aside over the years.

My first task is to support them to clear away the blocks to these innate gifts and heartfelt talents. So often we all hold the most profoundly important gifts within us, but because someone told us we weren't smart, capable, worthy, old, young, beautiful, handsome, or efficient enough, we put our precious gifts into a box and sealed it up tight, hoping we'd never feel hurt like that again.

Designing a life on purpose means more than burning maps; we need to forgive everyone whose words and actions misled our hearts and reclaim what is ours. This is an essential part of our life's design. Forgiveness is *powerful* alchemy.

Although we may believe we've hidden these gifts away for good, they are still with us, sneaking out when our defenses are down, radiating their goodness onto the people around us. That's why we're surprised when people compliment us on our presence, our voice, our capacities, and our unique potential. There's so much we don't notice until it's felt and seen within another.

These gifts don't have to become a full-time job. They don't need to earn money right away. They don't need to be shared publicly until you're ready. You can't climb a mountain in one leap.

In fact, the freedom you'll feel by pursuing a passion on the side that you don't desire to make money from or share with others is enormously liberating. You can have as many hobbies as you like that give you quiet satisfaction. And if there comes a time when you want to design a new path, expand the one you're on, or add deeper fulfillment to your life, ascertaining what gifts you're already honing or utilizing can provide you with all the guidance you need for designing the new direction you're heading toward. In the soul prompts that follow, I've listed a few questions to help you dig deeper into this, but the key to knowing what you're really good at *and* what is needed from you is honoring what you love doing that also helps others.

And if I were to intuitively guess, I'd say ... *you're already doing it.*

Never underestimate the way you dance through life or the craft you do for fun on a Sunday morning, the way you appreciate animal tracking or macramé, drawing with neon paint or writing haiku, making feathery crafts or beating a drum, holding hands with laboring moms or praying for the deceased, saving tigers or writing code, mentoring teenagers or designing daybeds. If you're in love with your craft and it contributes to, sparks a smile in, heals, inspires, or empowers others, then you have a real gift of service. If you have something to share that makes life more beautiful, simpler, easier, or more interesting, then it's worth taking a close look at how you already do this and expanding it in any way that feels aligned with who you are and how you connect with those around you.

Your gift doesn't have to be your main job, nor does it have to be a lifelong journey. Simply honor it and weave it into the design of life with love and attention. Embrace your gifts without attachment and let your purpose be fluid. Expect miracles and abundance as you share yourself openly, compassionately, and honestly with others.

As you design the purpose of your most daring dreams, let go of what everyone else is doing. Call back your energy from comparison. There's no need to look around you. Open your heart. Look at what you're already doing. It's there.

Ignite the spark already within.

· PRACTICE ·
Gold Within Soul Prompts

This process is golden, alchemical. The main idea here is to forgive others for interfering with your natural purpose, then see how you can create newness from this fresh state.

Answer these questions in a notebook with an open heart and mind. If there are any blocks to accessing the gifts and talents you had when you were younger, lovingly look at where you may have hidden them because someone told you you weren't "good enough" at something you loved, or because it wasn't the "right" thing to do.

1. What did you spend hours doing as a child? As you answer this, look at *all* the ways you entertained yourself, connected with others, daydreamed, crafted, or lost yourself during timeless afternoons.

2. What subjects did you enjoy most—or want to do but never had a chance—as a teen? Without thinking about grades or awards, and without relying solely on feedback from teachers and parents, simply feel into your teenage self and recall what you enjoyed most at school.

3. What did you excel at in your early jobs? What roles were you guided into by perceptive employers or your natural abilities? What aspects of your personality—such as leadership, organization, friendliness, patience, eagerness, and integrity—were appreciated the most?

4. Take a moment to consider all you've written down and notice how you were perhaps blocked, confused,

or distracted from pursuing what you loved. Even if you can't remember why you hid your talents away, just noticing what is there—and still within you—is incredibly liberating. Send out a wave of forgiveness to everyone who kept you small, predictable, unfulfilled, or unable to follow your heart. Send it to those who come into your awareness. Send it to the past versions of yourself. Keep sending it until you feel a shift.

5. Consider your current life and what makes you good at what you do now, even if you don't love it. How can you take that talent and dream it into something new and aligned with your heart? What interests do you have outside of your job? List them all and take note of what your heart is calling you to spend more time doing.

6. Look at everything you've just written down and see how many gifts and talents make themselves known. Without overthinking the process, start designing your purpose according to your creative heart. You may write related words in circles and draw arrows to kindred ideas. You might underline gifts and talents you've forgotten about and wish to cultivate. Dream jobs may make themselves known.

7. If there's something that your Soul is calling you to do, go ahead and do it. You're still in the design process of this book, but life might be calling you to jump already and take the job, do the course, or call a particular person. Go ahead. If you're hesitant, play with this for a little while longer. Dream and design all you desire. But when the nudge gets solid, it's time to act.

8. Keep writing, drawing, and playing with your ideas until you feel clearer and more connected to who you are. As you go about your day, notice how your gifts and talents sparkle and shine through all kinds of subtle or noticeable ways.

HONOR THE UNFOLDING IN EVERY ENDING

What we so often overlook as we experience endings in our life is the sweet and subtle grace of a beginning sprouting from within the resolution of what once was. Flowers are the perfect teachers to show us the gift inside every ending.

· JOURNEY ·
Wildflower Therapy

After your heart-opening, profoundly healing climb on the mountain, see yourself coming into a field of wildflowers full of windblown, raucous colors. Each flower—grown from a lineage of divine beauty—plays with your senses. Nature's perfume swirls around you, colors hypnotize you, bees cast spells as they dance from bloom to bloom, and the softness of each petal touches your sun-blessed skin.

These flowers are your teachers today; they have brought you here to show you how simple, gorgeous, and rich their glorious life is.

In their presence, you feel exquisite, radiant, and slowly you sense stale energy leaving your field. Without needing to know what is leaving, you feel the tension and let it go. When all the dense energy has left your aura, you relax in a peaceful state.

Within the fresh expansiveness of your being, you notice that through the shedding of stagnancy, you've made space for new, more powerful, and sustained vitality. A fire of strength and alchemy streams through you from the core of your being, each flicker a cleansing, pulsating, radiating beam of light.

Opening your arms wide and breathing in fresh lifeforce to fan the flames, you feel a tickling sensation in your hands. Peering down, you see soft seeds swirling around your palms. The flowers around you are showing you that life is a beautiful and messy cycle of taking root, growing tall, blooming petals, showering seeds, letting go, and renewal.

As you fling the seeds into the wind for them to grow roots in a new home, you see how divine the process is: *the beginning is always in the ending.* Your courageous heart glows strong as you see with fresh eyes the kaleidoscope of color and beauty all around you.

THE BEGINNING IS ALWAYS IN THE ENDING

For many years, I was in charge of a stunning food provedore. This place was wall-to-wall deliciousness. Bronze-extruded pasta sat next to green picholine olives; Sicilian extra-virgin olive oil was cracked open near large black canisters of sublime French tea; mouthwatering chocolate came wrapped in the most elegant packaging; Italian mustard fruits squished perfectly together in glass jars; Kangaroo Island honey glistened in the light through the window; and perfectly pungent truffles were flown in at the beginning of each season. The cheese room was my haven; the planet's greatest cheeses were stacked in a temperature-controlled room in the center of the shop, beckoning me all day, every day. It was a place like no other, one that catered to my every gastronomical whim. These days I prefer as much of my food grown as locally as possible, but in my twenties, I was naively oblivious and soaked it all up with hungry abandonment.

Each day I welcomed chefs and restauranteurs, food editors and stylists, culinary writers and authors, and many who, just like me, had a deep curiosity about food and valued the best ingredients. I gladly and gratefully talked about the ingredients we sold all day—where they came from, why they were extraordinary, and what to do with them to make them *sing*.

My earliest memories are all some kind of sensory experience involving food. My mom is a highly intuitive and experimental cook, and I gladly spent most Saturdays as a kid helping her in the kitchen. Whether we were whipping up walnut brownies or a roast chicken, blackened trout or Russian pierogi, the best part was tasting it with Mom. I appreciate how food can bring people closer together, whether they are cooking it, eating it, shopping for it, or reminiscing about it. After a childhood that revolved around great food and ten years working in restaurants, this particular job at the provedore was perfect for me in every way, though after a few years I could no longer ignore the voice within that urged me to write for a living.

Every time I ate at an inspiring restaurant, I would write a review the next morning. I never showed anyone; it was all just for fun. In my notepad, among these reviews, I had a bucket list of foodie destinations, my favorite original recipes, and design ideas for a café I wanted to open. I felt a deep satisfaction writing about food, and over time, the urge to be a food writer grew strong.

One day, a customer came into the store, looked me right in the eye, and asked me when I would *finally* become a food writer. I laughed in shock; he had seen straight through to my deepest passion, the one I couldn't admit to anyone. He told me how much he loved the way I composed recipes on the blackboard each week and how eloquently I described the meals I ate. He returned the laugh, but his eyes were serious. He *knew*.

The beginning is always in the ending.

Within a week, I quit my job and found two part-time positions elsewhere—one at a sumptuous Italian restaurant, the smallest I'd ever worked in, and the other in a tiny food store and café; that would give me enough time to find a job as a writer. Six months later I became a personal assistant to an associate publisher of Australia's largest publishing house. During my time as an assistant, I met incredible food editors and witnessed the dedication they gave to their careers. Their obsession with food was beyond anything I could *ever* commit to. With that understanding—knowing that I wasn't meant to have a solitary focus on food—I pivoted and expanded my vision to encapsulate many other aspects of writing. Eventually I became a health and beauty editor for a national magazine. I wrote about psychology and well-being, beauty and fitness, interiors and gardens. While working at this job, I received the deepest sense of fulfillment and joy. I wrote every single day, I was paid for it, I learned about the creative production of magazines, and I met some of the most loving and gifted friends I still keep close. I was also thoroughly challenged in this role, but it sharpened my skills and talents as a writer beyond what I could have imagined.

Three years later when my position was made redundant, I had already begun spreading my wings in preparation for my next creative career move: working as a freelance writer for many different magazines, which ultimately allowed space for me to write my first book.

The beginning is always in the ending.

Seeds for your future are already sown in—and fertilized with—the decay and ash of each ending. They come to life in the light that bursts through the dawn. Newness blooms incessantly out of the old debris. It always has. It always will.

When your job, hobby, or pursuit no longer feels relevant or satisfying, it's not because you're not good enough anymore, it's because your energy is no longer aligned with it. That might show up as boredom, stress, or exhaustion. It might look like you're not "performing" anymore or that other people aren't connecting with what you're doing. This is your heart telling you through your body and circumstances that a shift needs to occur.

For those on the spiritual path, the need to pivot is so much greater because as you evolve and enlighten, you need your career to match your ever-escalating vibration. If you're clearing blocks, expanding beliefs, and rising into the highest version of you, your outdated job may feel constrictive and uncomfortable if it's not at the same level.

If you are in the midst of an ending along your career path, know that the beginning of the next stage is awakening within. Perhaps there's a person you've already met whom you'll be creating magic with. Maybe you've been infusing your gifts and talents with a loving dedication, and those around you are intrigued to see you dance with these energies. It's possible that the intuitive energy of your heart has picked up on the presence of an opportunity that's absolutely meant for you or the chance for you to start your own business. Somehow the dream seed is slowly growing roots.

When you sense a misalignment in your field or feel an ending is close, go back to the drawing board. Rework your vision or create a new one. Design your next step rather than hoping it will happen for you by chance. Keep dreaming, designing, and knowing that the Universe is supporting you *always* and celebrating your every wildhearted move.

Keep moving forward, like the seeds of a flower in the breeze, trusting the promise of newness even if it cannot be seen yet, and traveling the highest path with your heart wide open.

· RITUAL ·
Intentionally Seeding a New Dawn

As the earth dawns a glorious new day for humanity, there's a lot of messy degeneration and untethering of the old ways. Each of us is a microcosm of the macrocosm. In our personal lives, the brave and necessary letting go of the old is allowing it to dissolve on a planetary level and make way for loving, fresh, harmonious life.

As we look around from the perspective of love, we can see the precious new growth sprouting right in the middle of the patriarchy's last breath.

So often, our focus is external. We're presented with endless rounds of drama and chaos in the media, and we look for it elsewhere, addicted to the need to fix it or the adrenaline rush it provides. What we need to assist with the transformation of humanity is a personal inner focus. To look within, accept what's there, humbly acknowledge our responsibility, and allow the outdated and misaligned thoughts and energies to transmute as newness comes flooding in like the rising sun.

To honor this, set a date with the wildflowers each month to plant new seeds in your garden. You might want to sow flower seeds in a pot to give away as a gift or place them straight in your garden.

During the ritual, be sure to add some compost and ash to the soil and say this invocation or create your own:

I seed this new life, a fresh being of love for this New Earth
Planted with loving hands, surrounded by alchemical decay
May it be blessed by the elements and grow beautiful

May it find its own way to live and breathe, sovereign and strong
May it inspire and animate new dreams in my life
May we grow and flourish together in harmony and symbiosis
May we be abundant in all we give and receive
And so it is.

Chapter 5

CONNECT TO YOUR HIGHEST PURPOSE

*"You cannot take responsibility for how well another accepts your truth; you can only ensure how well it is communicated …
how lovingly, how compassionately, how sensitively,
how courageously, and how completely."*[8]
—NEALE DONALD WALSCH

It's not always possible to take a few days or weeks to go into seclusion and consciously design a new purpose. It helps, but it's not necessarily feasible every time we desire the quietude. The way through this is to learn how to redesign or relaunch your visions, creations, and purpose as you flow through life. In taking easy pauses to get curious about each step toward truth and what that looks like in each moment. To create space every day for a softer, stronger, more sacred approach.

As you deepen your appreciation of yourself and the precious, powerful heart that beats at your core, you evolve on your spiritual path. And as you design a purpose that can evolve with you, it's important for you to keep a higher perspective, hold your truth

---

8. Neale Donald Walsch, *Conversations with God: An Uncommon Dialogue, Book 2* (London: Hodder and Stoughton, 1997), 16.

lightly, lean toward optimism, and curate a team of support when you need it most.

SEEK THE HIGHEST PERSPECTIVE

While we're in the midst of the dance of life, it can be hard to see it from a wide enough perspective to have a greater understanding of *all* that's going on. When we pause to view life as a witness from above, there's less to worry about and more to love.

· JOURNEY ·
Higher-Dimensional Songbooks

Picture yourself awakening from a long sleep among flowers and bees, the sun streaming through your view and lighting up the mountain you're heading back over on your way home. You bid farewell to the flowers, wishing them well. Then, as you reach the other side of the mountain, about halfway down, you look over your campsite and community from a higher elevation. You see how precious and perfect each friend is, how valued they are. You notice how lovingly the trees bow in the breeze to the collective as the sun kisses each shoulder. You feel a gentleness sweep through you as you appreciate what matters to your heart.

As you watch the morning rays enveloping the sky, your ears open fully to the tones of distant birds. They sing a range of harmonies from a higher-dimensional songbook; the lyrical messages sink through your skin, like droplets of melodic light from the Great One.

The vibration of your admiration ripples through the atmosphere, and soon the birds gather at your feet. You focus on the white light of your heart, sending gentleness to the birds. Soon birds of all sizes and colors, vessels of feather and song, creatures of comfort and hope, come to your arena. They sing resoundingly all around you, and you sing along with laughter and joy.

Your delight turns to something deeper as your inner ears open to the wisdom and guidance of each bird. These birds look so small and simple to your outer eyes, yet they feel like ancient wisdom keepers to your inner ears as they share their divine messages, saluting you for your wide-open heart and capacity to receive fully.

Songs resonant with the wisdom of a thousand lifetimes stream through you. Your light codes are activated and bliss saturates your whole being.

With your eyes closed, you imagine flying into the next version of you, infused with the highest, lightest vision and direction in your heart.

Gifts of a Higher Perspective

There's a higher perspective that's available to us in every moment. Rising into this outlook provides inspiration, illumination, appreciation, and peace.

Sometimes I sense this energetic altitude when I place my hands on a tree, swim in the ocean, witness a spicy sunset, surrender to a sound healing, look into the eyes of a conscious other, soak up the fragrance of a rose, or listen with my heart to the sweet song of birds. Other times I intentionally imagine a higher perspective by perceiving my human self from the realm of the clouds.

Birdsong is a gift from the Divine. From a human perspective, birds just warble at each other with messages regarding food, mating, intruders, and territory. From a higher perspective, they are earthly angels. And even when we can't see them, their song flitters through the atmosphere and lightens our heavy load.

Although each bird has their own particular medicine—owls for higher wisdom, crows for mystery and magic, hummingbirds for lightness and play—the overall message from birds is to pause, listen, and see life from a fresh point of view.

This is essential when it comes to traversing a purposeful life. We spend a large amount of our energy, focus, and time dealing with everyday events: taking care of children or other family members, communicating with our community, tending to our home and garden, working at a job, exercising our beloved body, cooking and eating, paying bills and keeping ourselves organized, and the other repetitious matters of life.

Taking a precious moment to embrace the *gifts of a higher perspective* can provide relief, a renewed passion for what we love, a sense that all is well and occurring in divine timing, and a clearer understanding of where to go next.

One of the first aspects that may become obvious from this angle is what *isn't* meant to be in your life and knowing what action to take to clear it out with love. As you evolve, you naturally raise your vibration. As your overall vibration rises, you'll notice situations, ideas, opportunities, jobs, and people who don't align with your realm. A higher perspective will bring this clearly to your attention and help you let it all go.

Some of the most important work I do with clients who are looking for a clearer purpose is to bring their personal blueprint to life from a higher outlook. This is a visual exploration of everything in their life that they are pouring their energy into—what is lighting them up and what needs to go or be outsourced. When all aspects of their life are clear, there's space that can become fertile ground for what their heart has been calling them to do, whether that is crocheting, starting a nonprofit business, growing a vegetable patch, learning a new skill, establishing an open-hearted community, or simply having more time to relax and savor life.

When you take a bird's-eye view of your life, you're also able to work with bird medicine—it's a natural synchronicity. Opening your inner ears to the mystery of birdsong is like opening your heart to the magic of your Soul's song. Your Soul is sharing its divine wisdom with you at all times, and, like birdsong, it radiates brighter when you pause, listen, and honor what comes through.

The gifts of a higher perspective are the capacity to lovingly perceive and design your life from a softer, stronger, and wiser view. You can create more space in your life by letting go of busy-ness and anything that drains you; this will give you enough time and energy to bring life to the design you're creating.

Your appreciation for what matters to your heart will grow exponentially when you access a refreshed outlook on life. And the grand design of your purpose will spring to life in all kinds of unexpected ways.

Sometimes life requires you to spread your wings and fly higher to *receive the gifts of a greater perspective.*

· PRACTICE ·
Expanded View Soul Prompts

Looking at life from a higher perspective is a practice I have done personally for many years and is an inspiring exercise I encourage my clients to do, either at the beginning of a new phase in their career or at the start of each year. Here's how I do it.

1. Take out a large piece of paper or a double page in your journal and some colored markers.
2. In the middle of the paper, write your name. All around your name, write everything you do in keywords, such as *social media, designing, writing, gardening, playing a musical instrument, composing, producing, shopping, website*

updates, packing, and *client calls.* Keep it simple to make the view from above crisp and clear. Do this exercise from your heart as well as your head; let them work together.

3. Notice how the energy in your body feels when you tune in to each of these parts of your work life. Take your time tuning in and be honest. With everything that doesn't bring you satisfaction, abundance, or joy, see if you can let it go. If you can, cross it out. Otherwise, see if you can outsource it to another—write down who might be able to help and how. If you can't let it go or outsource it, ask yourself if it's possible for you to attend to this with greater acceptance and ease. Bless it daily and allow it to transform into a more meaningful and enjoyable aspect of your life.

This can be a powerful and interesting exercise even if you work for someone else. It may nudge you toward a conversation with your boss or business partner about what you'd like to change in your everyday role, it might inspire you to look elsewhere for a job that fills your page—and your life—with exciting ideas and tasks, or it might make clear that this job you're currently in is fulfilling and joyful in ways you hadn't previously noticed.

There may be parts of your life that need amendment rather than removal. Make notes that help you feel more expansive and simplified. Observe the aspects that bring you the most happiness and fulfillment and dive into them regularly.

When you have completed the first part, take a fresh page in your journal and answer these questions.

- What can you see from this perspective that you haven't noticed before? What has been a surprise during this process? How does it make you feel?

- What are you unexpectedly grateful for? How has your perception of your tasks and roles shifted?

- What desires or dreams would you like to add to your purposeful design? Is there something that is longing to be part of the highest plan for your life? Is there a dream you haven't acknowledged that you'd like to make space for?

- What else is your heart calling you to do in service to your community? How do you enjoy relating to others? Would you like to volunteer, work casually at a place that interests and excites you, or host workshops, retreats, or talks locally?

- What might be missing from a feeling of complete fulfillment that is making itself known now? Is there an empty space and you don't know what belongs there? Take a minute to ask what your heart wishes to share about this. You might want to ask your heart to show you over the next few days what is ready to come to life.

- What important information does your Soul have to share about your life from a higher view? Take a deep breath and acknowledge the presence of the light within. Ask your Soul what it sees for you. Note whatever comes through you.

You don't have to do everything you write down—you're just giving yourself permission to sketch out your current life so magic can flow from there. Have fun with the process. Notice what comes up for you in the next week regarding this design. Take time to redesign the whole or parts of your purpose from a higher perspective whenever you feel stuck, unbalanced, resentful, bored, exhausted, or out of sync with love.

HOLD YOUR TRUTH LIGHTLY

Truth is powerful and important, but never definitive or "right." The more fluid you are with your envisioning and designing processes, the more you remain open to modifying, deleting, or reconstructing the truths that you hold strong. When this fluidity meets with the strength of inner conviction, your foundation can carry you wherever you desire to go.

· JOURNEY ·
Receiving and Sharing in Truth

Imagine coming home to your camping ground, surrounded by your beloved community, excited to share what you experienced with the birds on the mountainside. In your ecstatic rush to express your encounter, something you've never experienced before, you interrupt discussions, talk over others, and insist that people hear what you need to share.

By the time nightfall comes, you've exhausted yourself and frustrated others with your tenacious and inappropriate dialogue. You were so caught up in this higher way of seeing and sensing that you didn't ground yourself when you arrived back at camp. You fall asleep and dream about birds. During one particularly insightful dream, a bird claims your attention by being impossibly still and grounded while others are flying all around.

In the morning as you journal with your dreams, you realize there's an important message enfolded in them about holding your truth close, not pushing your opinions onto others, and seeking a feeling of security with Mother Earth rather than from wanting others to agree with you.

You decide from now on, as best as you can, to hold your truth lightly.

After breakfast, you take a walk to the nearest tree. You wrap your arms around its immense core and breathe in luscious, grounded, strong energy. When you feel more inwardly assured that your view and truth are important, even if they're never shared with your community, you head back to camp with offerings for lunch.

During your afternoon work in the vegetable garden, a magpie comes to sit with you. Silently you send it love, welcoming its presence and wisdom. A friend notices your connection and asks what message the magpie has and inquires about your experience on the mountain. You gently reply with a few words of wisdom from the magpie and what you gained from your elevated experience. You tell them of the way the feathers cleared your aura, the way the birdsong brought euphoria, and the precious meaning of perspective.

You learned from your insecure connections yesterday that you only wish to share your experience with others from now on as a humble storyteller, not to insist that others pay attention or adhere to your way. You've always known the intrinsic power of storytelling—the way it takes people on a journey, opens their senses, and inspires them personally. Now you have a more visceral understanding of this power and how it teaches others lovingly and indirectly to listen to their own Soul.

Soon there are a dozen friends, all who seem to have forgotten about yesterday's clumsy attempt at connection, surrounding you in the garden, wanting to know more about your day on the mountain. You share your adventure with a renewed spirit. Everyone smiles in delight as you express yourself colorfully, sensually, breathlessly, and humbly.

Your communion and healing with the birds is something so innocent and simple, yet you will never forget it. Now it has been shared in detail and will be passed along to others with their own perspective woven between the words and within the energy of the tale.

Your soaring heart grows even wider thanks to the presence of a deeper humility. Truth feels empowering to share lightly. One look around at the group before you, and you can already see the way you've inspired them simply by being grounded and secure in your sharing.

TRUTH IS A PERSONAL OPINION

I wasted far too many conversations in my youth trying to convince another of my opinion, not valuing their own thoughts as true and perfect for them. I didn't understand the impact of my disrespect until I became better acquainted with the ways of my ego.

I learned that my loving Soul is simple awareness, unattached to all opinions and thoughts, and my ego is addicted, attached, and proud of all thoughts, opinions, and judgments.

Shortly before I became pregnant with my son Lucas, now twelve, I read *A New Earth* by Eckhart Tolle. Through Eckhart's profoundly eloquent and gentle explanations, I was able to recognize how powerful it is to preserve my energy by allowing others to live freely and turn my attention to mastering my own journey by simply witnessing my ego.

In his book, Eckhart writes, "What a liberation to realize that the 'voice in my head' is not who I am. Who am I then? The one who sees that."[9] This line completely changed how I moved through life. As a thoughtful surveyor of life, a Gemini, a writer, I think *a lot.* And I used to cling to many of those thoughts as universally true and *so important.*

To move my presence from within the thoughts to behind them—so that I could be a witness and not caught up in them— was comforting. It helped my relationships because I was able to be more present with the other. My ego could throw around thousands of compliments, judgments, and assessments about the person or the situation, but often I would find myself in the inviting portal of the present moment, listening with my whole being.

"Can you look without the voice in your head commenting, drawing conclusions, comparing, or trying to figure something out?" asks Eckhart.[10] It's still a work in progress, but it's one of the most important processes I've discovered in my life.

To be present is to get to know your presence. And in your presence lives and breathes your purpose.

A few years after I read his book, I saw Eckhart speak in a large inner city auditorium in Sydney. I was speaking to my husband before the talk began, and without a cue or any direction, the *entire* audience hushed as Eckhart walked on stage. He sat in a chair for a moment without speaking, a glimpse of amused spaciousness on his face, and in that peaceful pause I could hear the entire Universe. Such is the power of presence when the ego is left backstage and the mind is free to be simply aware.

The present moment will expand your awareness beyond your mind and body to an infinite field where all wisdom resides: the Akasha or Akashic library. This higher-dimensional place of all

9. Eckhart Tolle, *A New Earth: Awakening to Your Life's Purpose* (New York: Penguin, 2005), 22.

10. Tolle, *A New Earth*, 240.

knowledge is only accessible in the present moment when you're clear in your mind. Here in the *Akasha*, a Sanskrit word meaning "sky" and "ether," you're able to find the truth, the essence, the higher wisdom of all you seek.

Part of my beloved purpose is sharing messages from Spirit, wisdom from the Akasha. As a former know-it-all, there's a huge temptation for me to step in with my own egoic ideas on situations my clients need help with. With this in mind, I call on Spirit before I meet clients and set my intention to be a clear channel for others and to access the Akasha from the highest source of light. As I visualize, design, and create magic with clients, I draw inspiration from the Source of all light, and the outcome is as wild and pure as can be.

However your purpose unfolds, it's helpful to know what your ego is up to each day. Some days it wants to create drama; other days, it wants so badly to be right. Your ego is the part of you that fears the worst, grabs hold of attachments, and points out the lack in your life. It directs you to play small and tells you that your abundance, your friends, your art, your sacredness, and your possessions are all flawed.

Your intuitive, insightful voice of love is calm, gentle, and kind. It sees all as abundant and whole. It relishes each moment without a single care. It wants what's best for you and is attuned to the highest aspect of you. It knows that *truth is only a personal opinion.* Your intuition wants to take your hand as you design the next layer of your purpose with optimistic freedom and insatiable hope.

Get to know your ego. Let it soften, and you'll find living on purpose and sharing your truth to be a smooth process. In this very moment, your purpose is alive and well. Right now, your heart is aglow with all the direction, guidance, and innovation you need to design a purposeful life.

The only truth is what you perceive and believe to be relevant and real in this moment. Your truth will flow over time as you learn and surrender; allow it to change. As you design each step of your purpose, be connected to, but unattached from, what feels true today, and let go of all judgments toward anyone else for their truth and wisdom.

Hold your truth lightly at all times and allow it to inform and design your purpose while your awareness grows in the space of your Soul's loving presence.

· RITUAL ·
Be Life's Witness

Living as a witness to life, rather than anchored too deeply into your ego's narrative, will create a peaceful and purposeful attentiveness in your being.

The next time you find your mind drifting into thoughts of judgment, attachment, or fear, imagine your focus moving into your heartspace. Feel a ball of energy that is golden, pink, and warm; expand this light until it fills your being and overflows into the field around you.

This golden light is the part of you that is connected to and part of Source. It's the eternal and truest part of you. Your body and mind are fleeting, here for one life. Your light is alive forever.

When you next hear your ego's insistent chatter, try these steps.

1. Notice what you're hearing and gently acknowledge it as coming from your ego. Embrace your ego as part of you and let the thought drift away.

2. Take a deep breath and let go of the thoughts and any associated emotions with the outbreath. Repeat a few times until you sense a lightness.

3. Feel the presence of your light like sunshine within and around your heart.

4. Feel the peace that comes with witnessing life from this place of expansiveness and awareness.

5. Remain in this gently illuminating space for as long as you need.

CONSCIOUS VALUES AND PEACEFUL PURPOSE

There are a few powerful ways to set down an anchor within your being as you walk through your wild and unmapped purpose. One of these ways is by knowing your values and staying aligned with them in everything you do. You get to define your values and decide what matters to you; with this attunement and awareness, life will flow with all you desire and need each day with less effort.

· JOURNEY ·
Sacred Ceremony in Nature

This adventure begins while you're scraping dirt from rocks one day.

You've come across a handful of large, curved, and perfectly placed rocks to use as a foundation for a rock pool. You pause to share your intention with the rocks and ask for their permission to make a healing pool with them. Taking your time with this process has strengthened your reverence for the land where you live. The rocks speak kindly to you, the birds come to see what you're working on, and friends come to use your nourishing soil for their projects on the land.

When the rocks are clean and the pool looks almost ready, you get busy finding clay where it lies in excess, soaking it in water, then draining it, pounding it, and spreading it between the rocks, filling each crevice with the thick medium that slips between your fingers and playfully drips all over you.

You leave the clay to dry in the sun, then on the next heavy rain, you check to see if it holds clear water. As you come to the pool, you find three of your dear friends soaking up the rock pool's medicinal rainwater. As you step in, your body feels so sublimely relaxed.

After a joyful while of soaking in the restorative healing, you hear the call of the Nature Spirits around the rock pool, asking you to create a ceremony for this place. You take a moment to get centered, then you use the water to bless yourself, your friends, and all who use this space for pleasure and healing.

You call on the nearby spirits of animals, trees, and wildflowers for protection for all who come to this water. You vow to take care of this land so long as you are here. You promise to listen to the spirits and pass on your sacred processes to all who live here.

You value the curative essence of nature, and nature values your reverence in return.

Appreciate Your Personal Values

If a higher perspective gives you the expanse and elevation of your truth, you'll find the depths and roots in your values. Underneath your everyday moments are your values, strong as a cluster of large boulders on top of which your purpose and existence flow along, or fragile as a scattering of pebbles, unsupportive and brittle in the face of a storm.

The values that are important to you are essential markers underneath your feet as you traverse your journey. *Knowing* your values anchors your truth into each step so deeply you can feel it. *Appreciating* them gives you the confidence to make all decisions accordingly.

I work and play in alignment with the values I hold close. It keeps me discerningly aware of what I bring into my life, my field, and whether it matters to me and my highest purpose.

My most treasured values are peace and play. I cherish these in all aspects of my life. My other important values revolve around these in some way, such as harmony, connection, freedom, calmness, balance, curiosity, fun, and expressiveness.

Getting to know, explore, and live fluidly within the container of my values has been profoundly helpful throughout my career. My life thrives when I pay attention to them, when I invite them to help me gauge where I'm at with my decisions. Often, honoring my values means establishing a respectful distance with people who have clearly opposing values and turning down opportunities where I would need to work against the values I hold close.

Whenever you feel drawn to set goals or design a purpose, write down the values you'll be holding close along the way. That way you'll only make choices that are beneficial to your mind, body, and Soul.

When you're in alignment with your core values, you'll effortlessly surrender anything that doesn't feel like a good fit or disrupts your balance. And you'll more easily call in abundance for your life in the areas that hold the deepest meaning for you.

Without connection to values, you may live habitually disconnected from your heart, as though stuck in unconscious ruts of doing what doesn't light you up. When you get to know and *appreciate your personal values*, you will feel the path of your purpose light up with opportunities that will take you to inspiring and enlivening places.

· PRACTICE ·
Defining Values Soul Prompts

Here's a practice to help you define your values and the ideals you live by.

When you have values to guide you in life, you'll make clearer decisions and find greater purpose. Knowing even a few values will help you when you're making any decision in your life, especially the important ones around your career. Here's how to unwrap your most important values:

1. Take out your notebook and write down at least ten of the principles that feel important to you, such as wisdom, friendship, diversity, vision, spontaneity, learning, nurturing, authenticity, bliss, compassion, independence, dignity, or transparency. Look up "values list" online if you need further inspiration.

2. Underneath each value, ask yourself why this is important. Keep asking this question until you get to the heart of why it matters. When you have that intimate connection with each of your values, you'll sense it in your whole being and relate to it within others. Energetically, you'll know immediately if a project, career, job, idea, or collaborator is for you.

3. Update your values each year. We're all changing, growing, and evolving, and what we value is going to shift the wilder our path becomes.

PURPOSE OF HOPE AND OPTIMISM

There are many levels of surrender. You can surrender your thoughts and give your mind a reprieve, you can surrender your emotions and lighten your heart, and you can surrender your body and allow yourself to rest deeper. All these are healing, restorative, and often blissful.

· JOURNEY ·
Visions of the Goddess

Your next adventure begins one morning as you wake feeling unusually on edge. Your mood is irritable, your body weary, your mind strangely isolated, and spiritually you're worn out. You're at a loss as to what has brought all this on, but in your quiet knowing, you sense this is a time for cleansing, releasing, and purifying.

You've heard that others in the community are feeling similarly, which helps you feel less alone. Yet you know this is an individual process, and the week ahead will require much solitary time. Your ego wants to blame other people's actions, the movement of the stars, and the fierce elements, but you know this is an inner transformative process that requires responsibility and softness.

As you think less and feel more, resist less and surrender more, you feel lighter. With an embodied consciousness, you take this lightness throughout the week into each compassionate interaction with others and nature. Hope flows from your heart in a moment of abandon, all fears dissipate into the presence of love, and slowly you come away from your edges.

During an evening of song and dance, you move your body spontaneously and sing the last of the dense fragments from your being. Holding hands with friends, the collective energy brightens with a shared sense of metamorphosis. As your body collapses into a heap of laughter and relief, you glance up at the sky.

The music and sounds around you fade as you focus with great awe on the colors dancing in the sky. It appears the angels have been dancing with you, celebrating your mutual healing. Soon, those around you look up. A hush comes over the circle, and everyone lies on the ground to watch this natural wonder.

The northern lights have come close to be in your presence tonight. They have met with you to dance with your rhythm, fly high on your joy, light up the cosmos with your song.

You feel ecstatic; the flowing purples, pinks, greens, and yellows merge with your aura and arouse new sensations—vibrations of hope, bliss, and freedom. These galactic goddesses move their divine light bodies through you, and your whole body quivers in sweet elation.

Visions of Aurora stay with you, the gift of lightness forever pressed into the inner sanctum of your memory.

THE VULNERABILITY OF HOPE

I'm a willful optimist. My thoughts about my life and future are unapologetically, unreasonably, and unconditionally hopeful, joyful, and light, even though I spent decades living with anxiety, even though I've felt the intensity of depression, and even though I drank more alcohol in my life than is advisable (until I quit in 2020).

I'm not immune to fear; it's so much more than that. I welcome fear—it's a doorway through which I can access even greater healing, hope, and peace. I'm a conscious and powerful transmuter of my fears and shadow aspects. I'm determined every single day of my life to heal and grow into the happiest, most grounded, expanded, and purposeful version of myself that I'm capable of. And I know full well that these capabilities are created with my thoughts, as are my limitations, perspectives, opinions, and judgments.

I take care of my thoughts. As I've mentioned, there are a *lot* of them. That's why I meditate; it's a few minutes of surrender that calms my thoughts and leads me toward more mindfulness. It's also why I don't drink caffeine (only cacao) and I focus on simple, nutritious food.

When I notice the edges of my capabilities, I don't give up; I see them as signs from my being that perhaps I have something to heal or tend to so that I may soften and stretch my potential into a more expansive expression of my being. Or perhaps the periphery of my potential is there for a more divine reason, a container provided by my Soul that will naturally expand as my consciousness grows. Either way, there's no pushing, only exploring and expanding.

I have always walked closely with hope. Hope is joyful and gentle around my edges. Hope is the energy that lures me toward the sun after a downward stretch. Hope takes my hand and enthusiastically shows me the possibilities before me. Hope spills out of my heart whenever I feel like a failure or I'm rejected, showing me there's a rainbow waiting over the mountain. Hope has a way of rounding up my concerns for the future and calling them into the present where they all disappear in love. Hope is my strength, and at the same time, it feels vulnerable and soft. It infuses my fierceness with a necessary gentleness and fortifies my openness with courage.

As you plan your next conscious career move, be sure to sit with *the vulnerability of hope.*

In her bestselling book *Daring Greatly,* Brené Brown riffs on vulnerability in such a tangible way that I have come to embrace moments of vulnerability in my life and career and then noticed in awe how they've become catalysts for some of the greatest conversations and decisions I've ever made.

Vulnerability is the reason I've been with my husband for twenty-two years. It's the reason I'm able to connect with my kids. And it's the reason I now live in the rainforest. Vulnerability cracked my heart open one Friday afternoon in September of 2021. My whole being felt soft and open, supple and raw, like a plaster had just been taken off. My heart was gently insisting that I speak to my husband about moving to the hinterland, so as soon as the kids were in bed, I made us a pot of tea, curled up next to him on the couch, and shared what had been on my mind all day: "I'm ready to leave this house when you are. I'm ready to move to the rainforest, in the valley between mountains. I love the beach and will miss it deeply, but my attachments to this house fell away today. I have no idea what shifted, but all I know is ... the mountains are calling. And I'm ready."

He didn't agree with me straight away, but that wasn't the point. I needed to share from within my vulnerability, and by doing that, I felt true to myself and my heart. After a few weeks of dancing around the subject, he agreed to wholeheartedly tango with the move. Three months later, we sold our house and bought a sixteen-hectare (forty-acre) property in the luscious rainforest of the Byron Bay hinterland.

Brené writes: "Vulnerability is the birthplace of love, belonging, joy, courage, empathy, and creativity. It is the source of hope, empathy, accountability, and authenticity. If we want greater clarity in our purpose or deeper and more meaningful spiritual lives, vulnerability is the path."[11]

In Brené's recent book *Atlas of the Heart,* she adds more texture to this understanding, writing: "There is no courage without

---

11. Brené Brown, *Daring Greatly: How the Courage to Be Vulnerable Transforms the Way We Live, Love, Parent, and Lead* (New York: Avery, 2012), 29.

vulnerability. Courage requires the willingness to lean into uncertainty, risk, and emotional exposure … Vulnerability is not weakness; it's our greatest measure of courage."[12]

To live from within the courageous embrace of hope and optimism, we *must* be vulnerable, first to ourselves, and then to those around us. We must only speak our truth, we must be willing to share what's hurting us or keeping us afraid, and we must be secure enough within ourselves to make unconventional changes along the way to reach the heights of fulfillment and abundance we are inherently capable of.

· PRACTICE ·
Letter of Hope Soul Prompts

Sit down in a peaceful space with your journal. Invite hope in, as though this emotion has its own presence (which it does—all emotions do), and write about the following:

1. Ask hope to share with you what it would like you to know about your purpose from its point of view. Write down whatever comes through your pen without pausing to edit or judge what flows.

2. Now, take some time to ask hope any questions you may have about your life. Allow hope to share with you all you need to know about these situations or feelings.

3. If you're feeling less than positive or optimistic about a situation, ask hope to show you the way to clear all negative and pessimistic blocks to your inherently

---

12. Brené Brown, *Atlas of the Heart: Mapping Meaningful Connection and the Language of Human Experience* (London: Vermilion, 2021), 14.

blissful nature. Your ego may want to interfere with the process; just uninvite it from the session and allow hope as much time as it needs to guide you back onto a higher, more peaceful and radiant path.

Whenever you are feeling low, try this journaling practice and take note of the changes within your being. Speak and act as though hope is in charge, not your cynical ego, and you will notice flowers of courage begin to flourish all over your internal landscape.

COMMUNICATE THE VISION TO THOSE WHO MATTER

Seeds awaken in the quiet depths of darkness. With nothing to show to the external observer, they subtly erupt, their newness unnoticed, their bravery without witness. And so it is in life: great sparks of creativity, bravery, insight, and newness take gentle root in quiet moments. Keeping your ideas to yourself at times can be a potent way of allowing them to gain depth before you share their radiant blooms.

· JOURNEY ·
Whispers of Creation

Imagine yourself connecting with new relationships in this community you share. You've spent time with everyone in groups and individually, sharing stories, experiences, ideas, laughter, song, and ritual.

Your allocated task during this moon cycle is to tend to the fire. Every afternoon you start the fire, build it up, and call the others round for dinner, conversation, and music.

On this particular day, the temperature drops right after lunch, and you feel as though everyone would benefit if you built the fire earlier than usual. You're ready to take your daily afternoon walk to collect food and kindling, only today, unlike most days, there's no one to join you. As you walk on your own, surprisingly grateful for the peace and serenity of your own company, the afternoon stretches out like a treasure for the senses. On your own, you hear the rain differently, like a symphony; the scent of flowers comes to life under your nose; the layers of clouds, and eventually the sun, become a silent movie of exquisite textures and light.

Your thoughts soften; your body feels alive, stronger, bolder, more alert.

As you come home to your firepit, you create a fire from a highly intuitive technique. You chop wood, snap sticks for kindling, arrange pine cones, and build the earth element into an entirely new shape. The fire comes to life quickly, and as you relax alone beside it, visions begin to appear within the silent alcoves of your mind. You see yourself as a vastly skilled healer, using the higher-dimensional healing flames invisible to human eyes to alchemize the pain and emotional blocks of others. As you absorb these images, you realize you've caught a glimpse into your past and future as one who sees pain in shapes and colors and who tends to it with the element of fire through transmutation and Source energy.

When the visions begin to fade, friends arrive to sit with you, rubbing their hands with appreciation at the fire you've created early on this cool evening. They come in reverence to your craft, as the flames are not only larger and warmer than usual, but they also have an otherworldly aspect to them that no one can quite articulate but everyone feels deep within.

For the rest of the evening, and many more to come, you hold your visions close to your heart, not sharing them with anyone.

They feel too wild, too incomplete, too personal, and too holy for them to be shared around the circle yet.

You'll hold them as long as you need to. You'll let the warmth of these visions sink into your bones, weave them with the knowing of your Soul, and create timelines never before considered.

As you fall asleep that night, a gentle smile flickers on your balmy face. The images you witnessed in the flames feel real, as though your Higher Self came to greet you today.

PAUSE FOR AS LONG AS YOU NEED

I struggle to keep secrets. Actually, I'm perfectly terrible at it.

If I receive good news, I must share the incredible joy with someone else to feel it fully. To dance and squeal and make all the celebratory moves. If I receive difficult news, I must share my despair with another, so it doesn't feel so tight and heavy.

I kept my early pregnancies mostly a secret, and I'm brilliant at keeping my client sessions to myself, but otherwise my life is an open book, metaphorically and literally.

As I evolve, I'm learning about the potency of keeping certain creative ideas quiet to build and expand their potential. While privacy might come naturally to others, it takes a gentle discipline for me to hold my cards close to my heart. This discipline is essentially what builds the energy of a new idea, I've found. I take time to sit with it, journal about it, ask Spirit for extra insights, and daydream about it under drifting clouds. It makes me feel giddy and over-flowing.

When I do share my adventures, schemes, and concepts, it's only with those I feel will support my dream, not critique or diminish it. If I desire feedback, I'll approach someone specifically who I believe can offer me an impartial and loving perspective. Otherwise, I'll happily share with others and allow the support around me to gently fan the creative flames, though the source of the heat will always come from within my potently creative heart.

It's not that I'm concerned about critical eyes or doubtful hearts—I have enough confidence in my work to know I will stubbornly make happen what is meant to happen, no matter what others say. It's that I choose to surround myself with successful and nurturing creatives, entrepreneurs, magic makers, game changers, and visionaries. When you surround yourself with the kind of people you admire and who admire you in return, you're constantly inspired to reach higher, love louder, live wilder, and serve deeper.

The next time you have a great idea, whether it's a creative way of sharing on social media, an original business plan, or a path of study you're embarking on, *pause for as long as you need* to build the energy of the precious flower bud and expand the potency of its wisdom within your field. Sit with it and let the magic come to you, pour through you, before you share it with anyone. This may only be possible for a few days, or you might want to simmer with it for a few months as you weave the details together. Take your time designing this newness without input from anyone, and only share it when you're absolutely ready.

As you create space to envision and design this idea, you might long for opinions and perspectives from other people. It might feel too challenging without it, or doubt might be getting in your way. In that case, call on your Soul family to hold the idea with you.

There are many benefits to sharing your journey of creation with your community, clients, and friends. As curious human beings, we love watching a creative journey unfold. There's no doubt that this can be inspiring and fun, but at times, a moment, a project, a conversation will feel too important to share. Perhaps it wants to remain in your heart forever or for a while.

When you work on something that's just for you, let the budding force of creation build a stronger confidence within you. Feel yourself deepen with every stage you move through privately, undisturbed, independently, and assuredly.

If and when you're ready to share it with others, you will feel all the more purposeful doing so.

· PRACTICE ·
Dream Design Soul Prompts

Perhaps there's a new beginning waiting to be birthed in your career. A flame that's been flickering for months, years, decades, patiently waiting for divine timing to strike and the winds of courage and clarity to build the force of the fire.

If there's an idea you've had a vision of, this is a strongly elemental and playfully visual way of kindling and stoking your dreams into a design that will come alight like a luminous fire. Here's how to set it up.

1. Open to a fresh page in your journal and draw the outline of a fire. Start with the rocks at the bottom, then the wood, flames, and then swirling wind all around. Be as creative as you'd like while leaving space between the lines. Use black pen or as much color as your heart desires.

2. Now, take some time to consider the dreams you have and what it would take to bring them fully into your life. Answer these questions on a blank page across from your fire, then circle the keywords that feel most important. Write each keyword on your drawing in the corresponding space; for example, the keyword for rocks needs to be written clearly on the rocks you've drawn.

3. What are the rocks—the stable, earthy foundation holding the space for your fire to be built? Perhaps the rocks are made of your current job that you'll keep until your side hustle makes enough money to live on. Maybe your rocks are deep self-confidence in your abilities as you step into this dream. It could be the intention that's flowing from your heart. Consider what you are depending and leaning on, within yourself and around you, for this dream to fully alight.

4. What is the wood you require, the fuel for this new purposeful adventure? Once you've established a foundation, you'll need fuel to get the fire going, as well as spare fuel to keep it burning for as long as you need it to. What and who inspire you? What excites you about this idea? What is the vision you're holding as you create your magic? What does it bring out in you? When the light of the project starts to diminish at some point in the future, when you're exhausted or unsure, what will help you get the fire burning again?

5. What are the flames made of, these lights that burn, radiate, warm, and illuminate? These flames are the purpose of your dream; consider what this is and how it affects yourself and others. How will your purpose play out? Who is working with you? Who will you share this purpose with? How does your inner warmth and luminous light radiate to others? How do you intend to make a difference?

6. What kind of wind do you desire to keep these flames burning high and bright but not too far in any one direction? When the fire is low, the right kind

of breeze can help it burn brighter. Sometimes this might look like taking time off, going on retreat, spending more time in nature, or connecting with like-hearted friends. A constant, gentle wind might also look like boundaries around work time, a fridge full of healthy food, an exercise routine that feels just right, or a wall of affirmations that keeps you positive and inspired.

7. Finally, how would you feel if this part of your purpose came to life? Why is this important to you? When you know why you're on this path and doing the work, you'll find it easier and clearer to stay with this fire for the long term.

This fiery design has so much to offer. A visual representation of what you're creating and how to keep it burning bright is priceless on your journey. I personally find the fire metaphor so helpful because purposeful creativity really is something that needs a solid foundation and daily attention. Keep loving your creations through mindfulness and appreciation, and you will constantly be connected to your highest purpose.

Chapter 6

ENRICH YOUR COURSE
WITH COURAGE

*"There is no limitation whatsoever in the structure of
your fundamental essence.
And you can, in fact, be anything you choose to be."*[13]
—RASHA

When you choose a life of wild creativity, vivid expression, personal empowerment, and intuitive pioneering, you will inevitably fumble, fail, and fall. There will be blocks to your path, in the designing, creation, and fulfillment of your purpose. Troubles, complications, and difficulties will tumble onto your trail, causing you to pause, reassess, and pivot where needed.

When you commit to living only from your fierce heart, you will know why these obstacles have come, how you created them, and how they are serving your greatest purpose. With consciousness, you can wrap your awareness around these issues and see them from all angles, compassionately softening the edges and opening to the gifts within them. With loving responsibility and mindful maneuvering, you will find a more energized and honest ambition *because* of the challenges that come your way.

---

13.   Rasha, *Oneness* (Sante Fe, NM: Earthstar Press, 2003), 294.

Begin with a bold vision, design with a brave heart, and soon you'll be creating with unreserved expression.

Planting Ideas on an Impulsive Whim

Creative ideas are uniquely spirited—there is energy within them that speaks to you and guides your route toward their creation. These spirits may need a little time and ask you to pause awhile in the darkness of not knowing, or they may be ready immediately, pressing you to pursue along the fastest route to their creation. When they come, you'll know. And when you sync with their spirit, you'll know *how*.

· Journey ·
Impulsive Impressions

As you continue along this meditative journey, imagine your beloved coming to you with a handful of seeds. They've been out in the fields, gathering them all morning from a dwindling patch of wildflowers. Your love would like to find the most generative space to sow them, a place so fertile and ripe that the flowers can take care of their own regeneration year after year. Together you set off around the land, guided by the direction emanating from within the seeds.

You haven't been looking for long when a heavy, dark cloud comes into view. While you don't mind walking in showers and rain, it looks like a potent storm is looming close. The seeds nudge your hands open and out they fly into the dirt right next to your feet, under a few rocks and beneath the daily arch of the sun. You lovingly and hastily sow the seeds, then run back to camp before the powerful storm cleanses the air.

In your tent with your love, you're inspired by the force of the deluge. Thoughts of boldly expanding your purpose come to the surface. You've been receiving new visions in your nature walks of creating a hut where you can teach what you've always known intimately and well: yoga and martial arts. You have a fondness and respect for these two ways of moving the body, clearing the mind, and expressing the Soul. Lately, as you've devoted more to a personal practice of both, you've received a few requests from your Soul family to teach them.

As the storm rages overhead, you pull out a piece of paper and begin drawing your temple. Simple lines merge with sacred geometry as the spirit of the temple and your Soul guide the process. When you finish, you say a blessing for this sacred space, calling on the Guardians of the land to help you create it with the highest intention. You pray that it may hold space for others to connect to and strengthen their mind, body, and spirit.

When you open your eyes, you notice that the storm has passed. Meeting with your community, you call on those who would like to help you source materials to build your humble temple. Within a few weeks the hut is complete. Although there were challenges along the way, you feel stronger and more connected to your spirit from the process. Finally, you crown it with a thatched roof of straw, reeds, branches, and heather.

A timetable comes together easily, and before your first class, you set off on a walk to prepare for the session in communion with the energy of the day. Walking toward the east, you honor the sun for its strong presence, you bow to the trees for their offerings and lifeforce, and you sit on a rock to appreciate the earthly support for bringing an important dream into being.

Placing your hands on the rock to stand up, you feel a gentle brush of petals on your fingers. With delight, you look down and realize the seeds you sowed before the storm last month have taken root, sprouted, and bloomed.

Like an impulsive, adaptable, and whimsical flower, you've found yourself in full bloom because you listened to the intuitive calling of your creative heart. With a deep, satisfying breath, you head back to the temple to be initiated on your first day as a teacher.

LIVELY SPIRITS OF CREATION

Creative ideas have a spirit of their own and are as much connected to you as they are to all of life. When ideas come your way, call them in closer, pull them toward you, ask your heart what it wants you to know through the mystery of creation. Don't ignore them or pretend you're not good enough to be the vessel, the perfect channel for their life. Ideas left to collect dust tend to lose their vibrancy and aren't always available for you to work with when, eventually, you're ready.

You may be asked to show up for a creative idea in ways that are confronting or healing. The idea may turn your life upside down or be easy and graceful. It may call on all your resources or be a sweet side hustle. You may need to involve your community or ride solo for the duration. There's no telling what kind of journey it may want to take you on, but if you're ready for a life of wildhearted purpose ... *say yes*.

I had never understood the notion that an idea was a muse, a *lively spirit of creation*—but it felt real in *all* my creativity—until I read *Big Magic* by Elizabeth Gilbert when my daughter was a newborn. I remember walking the house in circles with my sleeping babe in a soft carrier on my belly while I drank in page after page of delicious insight.

Elizabeth says about inspiration, "Be ready. Keep your eyes open. Listen. Follow your curiosity. Ask questions. Sniff around. Remain open. Trust in the miraculous truth that new and marvelous ideas are looking for human collaborators every single day. Ideas of every kind are constantly galloping toward us, constantly passing though us, constantly trying to get our attention. Let them know you're available."[14]

These words spoke right to my heart and opened a new, more creative and courageous way of communing with Spirit. Elizabeth reminded me that nothing is ever by chance, that ideas that make their way to you have chosen *you* specifically because you're the most ideal channel for their expression.

When I personally connected with Elizabeth at the Sydney Opera House when she was on a speaking tour for *Eat, Pray, Love,* I felt how deeply Elizabeth is entwined with her craft without taking it too seriously, and how she honors her gifts without putting them on a pedestal. I love her light and how it lights up everyone around her.

A few months before my babe Ariella was born, a surprisingly unexpected idea literally landed on my lap. I initially tried to disown the message from the *lively spirit of creation,* but eventually I succumbed to the idea; it was too rich, too magical, too obviously meant for me to give away.

The idea sprung out of a magazine that was resting on my knees with my pregnant belly protruding over the top. On a glossy page was a deck of everyday conversation cards. I said to my husband, "When will someone create a deck of conversation cards

---

14. Elizabeth Gilbert, *Big Magic: Creative Living Beyond Fear* (New York: Bloomsbury Publishing, 2015), 49.

that are soulful and *deep*?" He looked back at me and, not knowing what to say to such a redundant question, smiled and shrugged.

When I realized I was that "someone," I laughed at the question and the Universe for suggesting such a thing when I was about to birth my second child.

However, the persistent and virtuous muse wouldn't leave me alone, and over the months that followed, I unwrapped this gift slowly until it became a simple process that I felt able to take on with greater ease. The idea was to write fifty questions and leave it to a publishing company to design, print, and take care of the rest.

Shortly after my daughter turned two, *Soul to Soul* conversation cards had been published, the *lively spirit of creation* was pleased, and I was ecstatic. These cards were the first in a range of seven decks, including affirmation and oracle cards, I've created since then. And of all the sets I've made, this one has had the biggest impact by far.

As someone who mentors a lot of creatives and knows plenty of entrepreneurs, I've found that having an extraordinary idea land in your lap isn't rare—following through with it all the way to completion is. Perhaps it's a hand cream your muse wants you to make with sublimely healing ingredients, or a way of teaching kids the piano that hasn't been done before. Maybe the muse wants you protecting native bees or painting images of the Goddess. Honor the muse, commune with the creative spirit, get to know it thoroughly.

Some seeds need a pot of soil, a little sunshine, and a few drops of water to give them all they need for a full and blossoming life. Others need space to grow deep roots, lots of rain, and the right mix of minerals in the soil.

Like flowers, some creative ideas can be needy and testing, while others require just a little attention to grow into a life-changing opportunity.

When the muse comes, make it a cup of tea. Ask it questions. Let it lead the way. Give it what it needs without depleting yourself. Don't ignore it unless you're sure it's got the wrong person or the worst timing; then bless it and send it away without guilt. When you have felt it enough to know it well, when the collaboration is clear, sit down with it and create a design together.

When life gives you seeds, don't let them dry out while you overthink your process or undervalue your worth.

Sometimes you've really got to get those seeds in the ground before the storm comes.

· RITUAL ·
Scattering the Seeds

The creative muse lives inside the heart. They're the curious one who's always looking out for opportunities, ideas, and beauty. They'll whisper in your ear, sometimes with an accompanying nudge or a proper shove, whenever they sense creative abundance around you that aligns with your purpose. Most of all, they believe in you.

It may feel exciting, expansive, and unnerving. It's meant to. Great ideas will stretch you, call on you to reach higher into the ethers of your existence and create with high magic. You may not know how on earth these seeds could possibly grow into the sweet beauty captured in your imagination, but thankfully, it's not for you to know every minute detail—only for you to trust and follow.

This ritual will show you the infinite beauty and rich purpose of scattering seeds:

1. The next time you're in a garden shop, buy a pack of the most magnificent flower seeds you can find. Choose flowers that suit your climate, current season,

and the type of garden or pots you want to use. Take some potting mix home if you need it.

2. Sprinkle the seeds with a conscious intention. Cover them up with dirt, the veritable fertilizer of your past, and top with a few small crystals or pebbles. Give thanks, and make sure the flowers get enough sun and water each day.

3. Put the flowers near a space where you can sit with them or place a seat near the flowers in your garden. As the flowers grow, take a notepad and colorful pencils with you when you have a moment to sit with them. Write words or draw something to represent how each stage of growth feels.

4. In the initial stage of darkness and the unknown, write about your feelings when you're in this stage in your creativity and career. How does it feel before anything begins to flourish, before you receive feedback, or while you're working hard without a payoff?

5. As the first shoot pushes through the soil, and from this stage all the way until it dies, draw it in color pencils and write your thoughts, feelings, or where in your life you're at during this stage. What does growth feel like for you? How does the anticipation grow in your life before the bud of creation opens? What is it like for people to share their advice, opinions, and reactions with you? How do you take criticism? What happens when the bloom isn't quite the shape or color you expected? How do you manage expectations? How well do you rejoice in the full expansion of your creativity?

6. As the flower dies, give thanks and notice the often-overlooked beauty in the fading colors and softening petals. Allow this cycle to inspire your creative processes. Take the dead flower and use it as compost for a new plant, feeling into the cycle of life.

Let the flower be your muse and inspiration. Talk to it often; I'm sure it will send messages back to you in the most exquisite ways.

RISKING IT ALL IN THE REALM OF POSSIBILITY

The wild that you are being called into will redefine your goals and values, success and meaning, abundance and purpose. It will also challenge the notion that a career must be defined, consistent, stable, and certain to be satisfying. In nature, there is no certainty, no stability, other than what you carry within you and the assuredness of change. This untamed adventure is all about losing attachments to control and the need for restrictive stability while opening to the idea of unlimited possibilities.

· JOURNEY ·
Moving with the Tide

Feel how deeply you're belonging to nature on this purposeful adventure. From the regular visions you now witness in the light of the fire during a solitary moment, to the wisdom permeating the trees, and to the gentle medicine that flowers from your hands when you're one with it all, you're noticing how seamlessly you entwine with and express the essence of nature.

One day, on an unexpected jaunt to the ocean with friends, you experience this more intensely than usual.

The moment your feet land on the warm sand, you begin to experience a rush of past-life memories. Breathtaking moments from the ancient civilization of Lemuria lift your spirit high, and you lie in the morning sun, glowing with the activations that dance within your cells. Everything feels utterly peaceful, and the birds come to sing by your side.

Suddenly you're seeing your life in Atlantis, the period after Lemuria where technology ruled and many people became powerless. Confusion swirls as you remember how your intelligence was used against your values. This life was a shocking time of disconnection, taken away in a large wave over Atlantis and Mu, the paradisiacal land of Lemuria.

As you come back to your body, you notice the wind has amped up and is blowing sand in your eyes. You're irritated, resentful at that life of misguided service, fears surfacing and anger swirling. The more resentful you feel, the harder the sand rushes into your eyes, ears, nose, and mouth.

You're facing a sandstorm and about to reach breaking point. Somewhere, you hear a voice say, "Forgive." It's your precious heart, the eye of the storm, guiding you toward a more peaceful remembering of this life that was important to the lessons and growth of your Soul and humanity.

With the deepest access to courage, you place your hands on your heart and whisper in your mind, "I forgive you." This healing is directed toward yourself, all those who hurt and used you, and the divine force of nature that swept away the continents all those thousands of years ago.

As love colors your heart once more, the winds calm, and sand falls back onto the shore. Feeling at ease with most of the tension gone, you crave a saltwater swim. You approach the water, and the foamy waves kiss your feet. You look up at the luscious, overflowing ocean. You see wave after whimsical wave, and for the first time in your life, these waves feel safe, comforting, and healing. You bless the water and thank it for its medicine.

For so long, you've been intimidated by large surf—it's always felt dangerous. But the level of joy you feel as you swim with and jump over the swell of Mother Ocean today is liberating. You feel like a dolphin: naked, blissful, safe, and exuberant. The water reflects it all back to you in waves of uplifting energy. And as you vocalize your delight, you hear an echo. Turning around, you see the rest of your Soul family jumping in the waves with wide smiles, arms high, and eyes alight with joy.

Your body doesn't tire of this movement with the ebb and flow of the water. Together, as a pod of elated mammals, you surge with the waves all afternoon.

You Are a Naturally Limitless Being

Your essence, the light of your Soul, is eternal, immortal, multidimensional, all-knowing, and gifted.

When I tap into this ancient light within, this ultimate sense of expansion, I feel as though I can do anything, and I'm connected to everything. This feeling keeps me excited about my purpose.

When I *know* I'm *a naturally limitless being*, the Universe mirrors back to me again and again how limitless I am.

The beauty of creativity is that by its nature it's unlimited, boundless, and immeasurable. We are all creative; we all *create*. To create is simply to produce something … *anything*. There's a creative element in everyone's purpose, whether it's artistic, scientific, mathematical, spiritual; seen, unseen, written, sung; formulated, measured, intuited, dreamed; mindful, conscious, unconscious, channeled; serendipitous, planned, chosen, or guided.

Touching on this infinitely extensive realm is enough to be overwhelmed, but that's simply a reaction of the ego. Living into the bravest possibilities will feel "too big" for your ego because it knows and fears how wildly powerful it is for you to live creatively. But your true essence is not contained, it does not require stability, and it is aware of all the possibilities available to you right now.

You are not separate from your creativity; your creations come from your heart, tended to by your mind, and birthed through your physical form.

Playfulness and lightness are the perfect divine counterparts to the seriously inundated ego. Approach your creativity with a smile and a gentle touch, and you will find it opens up to you, like waves on a beach.

Just like the ocean, so vast and unchartered, the beauty and depth of unlimited creativity is available to all. Holding the belief that anything is possible in your heart, the place where all purposeful seeds are planted, will give you the impetus, the never-ending momentum, to move forward, onward, upward, over hills and mountains, between forests and fields of wildflowers, through caves and salty waves, under rocky outcrops and blazing sun, until you reach one destination after another. This joyful journey is never static, for life moves, ebbs, and flows onto the next dream, into the next adventure, as the ocean drifts and ripples for an eternity.

Within creativity, the human mind often detects—and runs from—risk. Risk has an edginess to it that's difficult for many to be comfortable with. But all opportunities involve some form of risk. We dance with risk all the time on our trails and treks of purpose.

When you know and believe wholeheartedly that what is meant for you will find its way to you, you'll never hesitate to accept or decline according to the impetus of your heart.

We're taught to believe that a truly creative life is risky, for it supposedly has no stability, and that a corporate job working for a large corporation isn't risky at all, because of its set hours and pay. This idea is based on an old paradigm that implies that stability—consistent pay/hours of work, a mortgage/home ownership, belongings, and a car—is necessary. This concept is loosening as we enter the New Age; we are rediscovering the joy and inspiration that comes from living creatively with supposed "instability," which is actually *possibility*. We are discovering that connection with community keeps us feeling steady, daily communion in nature helps us feel balanced, and we simply don't need to own as much stuff as we used to. Life actually becomes *more* purposeful this way because we create our own meaningful job description according to our great inner master (our heart), not an external master.

I understand the risk I've taken as a creative being working for myself, and I'm happy in the flow, knowing some months feel more abundant than others. Living in the forest means my attachments to "things" are looser than ever. I own much less than I used to, and I appreciate the joy that people and nature bring me instead. I *always* welcome abundance in all ways as I focus on the deeply soulful, satiated satisfaction I feel at the end of each day and especially at the end of each creative cycle. I am profoundly grateful that I get to shape my career intuitively, according to my creative ideas and the needs of my mind, body, spirit, and family.

In a very real way, I feel as though the bigger risk in my life would be to work for a company I didn't feel energetically attuned to. To work for someone else isn't something I'm immune to or ashamed about; it's something I would consider if it amplified my field through creative collaboration. However, I'm deliriously excited about the life I've created and the raw happiness that comes from living creatively in community.

Moving to a small suburb of Byron Bay in 2019 was a risk for our family and our creativity. What if we didn't find the community we were craving? What if we couldn't access all we needed for the life we wanted? What if the kids didn't feel supported? Thankfully, all we longed for has come to fruition. We have our community; we discover people to play and create with all the time. We access everything we need, and whatever is out of our reach isn't important, so I've discovered. Our kids love it; we found a school where they both thrive. We landed in just the right place for what we needed to heal after living in large cities our whole lives, and recently making the change to the hinterland has been powerfully expansive and deeply influential, even though living fully in the wild has felt risky, unpredictable, and vulnerable.

Wherever you work and live, however you feel, you're always an important note in creation's song. If you're part of a company that's creating ideas or objects aligned with your own purpose and you're able to contribute in a way that feels fulfilling, then you're living your purpose with each breath. Being creative doesn't mean you have to work artistically, on your own, or by some unraveling thread of uncertainty; it's listening to love and following the pulse within.

Feeling into the options, knowing the risks involved, and acknowledging your innate strength and resilience will cause vital energy to build. It's only when you deny the risk or repress the inner force of conscious creativity that you'll find yourself way out of balance.

There's no need to put everything you own on the line for one creative venture; have some money saved, ask for support, be proactive with what you need, do what you can to feel comfortable on your journey, and keep moving forward with a clear, conscious, confident outlook. You are unlimited in your potential and your wildest dreams are worth the risk.

· PRACTICE ·
Heartfelt Possibilities Soul Prompts

If your life is created by what matters to your heart, rather than on an external map that was given to you, then you may find risk to be not so challenging to your lifestyle. Simplify your life in whatever way feels good to open yourself to more creativity and less risk. Answer these questions in your journal to become more aware of your creative abundance.

- Where are you and what are you doing when you feel tapped into the unlimited possibilities of your Soul? Describe this in detail. If you haven't felt connected to your infinite potential yet, use this as an intention the next time you meditate or go for a walk in nature and then come back to your journal and write about the process.

- What dreams have you put on hold because they feel too risky? These might be obvious or subtle, so take your time with this. Keep coming back to this question every time an idea lands into your arms from the muse and consider the risk you feel is associated with it. When you look the risk in the eye, its power will melt, and you'll see the potential for the project; you'll be able to consider it all without fear and know if and how to begin.

- What have you created in the last five to ten years that stands out? Consider the houses you've lived in and how you made them feel like home. Write about your children, stepchildren, grandchildren, nephews, nieces, pets, and other beings whom you create life with. Detail your most important relationships and your creative role within them. Think about your work and all the small and big projects, assignments, jobs, ventures, connections, and items you've created or helped create. List anything else that comes to mind, from your garden to artwork or websites. Then look at this list and see what an incredible creator you are.

• What have you created along your spiritual path? List everything you can think of, such as deeper peace, sympathetic self-talk, soulful connections, profound healing, or a genuine connection to your Soul's purpose.

We are inherently creative, all of us as magical, imaginative, and expressive as nature.

INTUITIVE AMBITION AND A SENSE OF PURPOSE

Everyone has it within them to share their passions, lessons, and heart with others. The more we lavishly and humbly teach what we know, the greater we inspire.

· JOURNEY ·
Sacred Expression of Movement

In this playful, meditative realm, you hold a sacred belief that yoga is one of the most elegant expressions of the human form. Sacred geometry in motion, a portal to the higher dimensions. You also feel that martial arts is a collection of healing, protective, strengthening practices that shapeshift you into a creature of fierce grace.

Your physical practice keeps your body strong, while your meditation practice keeps your mind clear. Together, you have much experience and skill that you love sharing with others. Teaching yoga and martial arts to your community for many months has brought out a sense of accomplishment and contentment.

You feel as tall as the trees when you witness the individuals in your community connecting to a higher, more vibrant and elevated sense of holistic health. Your heart feels deliriously happy each time you gather with a group of people in nature and grow and heal together.

During mealtimes and gardening, dipping in the rock pool and building with your newfound construction skills, you chat blissfully about yoga and martial arts to anyone who has questions. Your genuine enthusiasm brings more people to your hut, and over time you create a variety of sessions.

After a year of teaching, your body needs a rest, and you take a month off. During that time, you glimpse a fresh perspective of your purpose. Sitting with a chameleon by the water in a moment of serenity, you receive a message from the shapeshifting lizard straight into your heart. The chameleon wants you to recognize how many facets of yourself you haven't seen yet. You've been teaching the same people who come to you in your hut, but you haven't reached out to the wider community, to those who are unable to leave their cabins and tents while they are recovering from injury or illness, the elderly, pregnant moms and new parents, or younger children.

You realize how many people look forward to your sessions as a special part of their weekly routine, but you're also now conscious of how valuable it will be—to your health and the health of many others—if you take the time to teach those who have become masters within these arts. Teachers for the teenagers, children, elderly, and new parents.

You bless and thank the chameleon for coming to you today with such an important message. Your mind is already full of visions of how you'll teach the teachers and share your gifts more mindfully to touch the whole community with your healing light.

Once you feel refreshed enough, you reschedule your sessions with a new design and approach. You call on those who have a particularly high aptitude for yoga and martial arts and, depending on their own gifts, talents, and skills, and invite them to learn the art of teaching to pass these methods on to the rest of the community.

Tuning in to the generous ambition and wider sense of purpose within you, you glow with possibility and inspiration. Moving forward with ease, you're aware of your connection to deeply satiated success on your path.

THE CYCLE OF AMBITION

Words resonate tangibly in my being. My most treasured job in this life is the one that created this book: weaving words together that feel good, inspiring, and true in the company of each other.

There are many words I use intentionally because of how I adore the way they feel in my being, such as *abundant, delicious, blissful,* and *love.* There are other words I avoid because their vibration feels dense and constrictive, such as *shotgun, deadbeat, killjoy,* and *annihilation.* As an empath *and* a writer, I love to feel my way through the garden of my work, wrestle out the thorns, and open the blooms as far as I can while keeping their integrity. This is an ancient gift I've carried with me for a long time, and in ambitiously honoring it, I feel on purpose.

Ambition has an interesting vibration to it. It used to feel like extreme hustling to me—like pushing your way to success no matter the cost. But the more I talk about purpose to friends and clients, the more the energy of *ambition* shifts. That's what I love about words: they can feel dense or light depending on how we view them, but this can change at any time depending on your personal frame of reference.

Some people have an outrageous amount of ambition, while others, almost none. Neither is good nor bad, but the way I've thought of my purpose is that I'm not so *ambitious*, more *intuitively driven* by my heart. I didn't think the two could come together; they felt like they lived on opposite ends of the spectrum of purpose. But the more I let the energy of *ambition* move around my field, the more I felt it land a little softer as it anchored into place.

The word *ambition* comes from the Latin word *ambitionem*, which means "a going around." When I sit with the idea of "going around," there's nothing inherently hustley about it. When it comes to sharing your gifts, going around feels necessary. Perhaps then, without ambition, you're at risk of staying still for too long and not reaching those who need your Soul's medicine; you're more likely to stagnate on the path of your purpose.

Going around feels cyclical, too. Honoring your cycles is imperative to being intuitively connected to your purpose. Within you lives a veritable Universe of cyclical cells, organs, and systems. Your breath and your life are cycles, too.

Having an intuitive understanding and expression of *the cycle of ambition*, then, seems to me like having the confidence to share your gifts, talents, offerings, service, and connectiveness in accordance and alignment with the cyclical flow of your being.

Like ambition, confidence can be seen as arrogance; it's another interesting concept that deserves to be understood intentionally and objectively in the realm of purpose. I've spent enough time in Canada and the United States to notice how genuine, warm confidence is part of the fabric of many societies there. Confidence is applauded, supported, and appreciated. After every visit, I feel more fully expressed and excited about who I am and what I do.

At home in Australia, confident people are often seen as abrasive, arrogant, boastful, patronizing, smug, or vain. They're "know-it-alls" who like to "show off." Looking at the laid-back Australian culture, I find it interesting how easily and incessantly we cut down "tall poppies" who grow high and radiate their beauty. We want everyone on an even playing field where no one stands out or is left behind. Aussies seem to have an underlying insecurity about success, which is why many creatives leave the country to create big, bold businesses overseas where they feel more supported. I appreciate how grounded and humble most Aussies are about their success, but I long for greater access to genuine confidence.

I believe we all *need* ambition. To meet aligned people, sell our beautiful goods, and market our wholehearted services, we need to *move around* our grassroots and online communities. And we *need* to be confident, whether it's celebrated or not, because when you know who you are and appreciate your significant role in your community, you'll have a more intimate sense of purpose.

Consider looking at your purpose as a *cycle of ambition*. When you learn something new—or heal something old—about yourself, you come to your purpose with renewed understanding, fresh energy, and the ability to share your medicine and wisdom in a more evolved way. To share this confidently, you need ambition—the momentum to go around and radiate your light so that those who need you can find you. You continue to do this until another shift occurs and you learn or heal, and the cycle begins again on another, higher level.

Your sense of purpose will expand and contract many times throughout your life. In the expansion phases, ambition will help you reach out to connect with others. In the contraction phases, nurturing stillness will hold you as you heal and rediscover yourself deeper.

If there ever comes a time when you feel the need to really hustle, to push past your limits for a launch, a target, or an important moment in your business, know you also have the power to balance this with remedial downtime once the hype has settled. So long as you listen to your heart the whole way, you'll discover a new level of confidence within yourself you may not have connected to before.

· PRACTICE ·
Ambitious Purpose Soul Prompts

Take out your journal and play with your understanding of the word *ambition* through these questions. Allow the process to unfold a new way of working with your purpose.

- What were you taught about ambition as a child? Was it light or dense, positive or negative, encouraged or suppressed, modeled or unavailable? What would your caregivers say about ambitious people?

- How does ambition feel to you now? Who would you describe as ambitious? Do you use the word as judgmental, inspirational, or neutral?

- How would you rate your confidence in your own abilities? Do you keep your confidence quiet or share it with others? Is confidence something that comes to you from feedback and encouragement from others or does it shine naturally through the core of who you are?

- What does your heart say about ways to grow your inner confidence? If you feel like you lack confidence, how can you fuel the fire of confidence within your being? What layers of doubt or insecurities can you let go of to allow your luminous confidence to shine through?

- In what ways do you follow your inner cycles when you work? Do you pause when you need to reset and nourish your energy? Do you focus and work productively and creatively when your energy is high? Do you push hard when your energy is low or procrastinate when your energy is ripe for creation?

- How do you intuitively navigate your day? Do you stick to a routine that works most days or do you flow according to the unpredictable nature of your curiosities? Do you check in with your mind, body, heart, and spirit at points during your day to see what you need to be healthy, happy, *and* productive?

- Here's a little extra design element to add to these soul prompts. Turn to a fresh page of your journal and draw a large flower. In the center of the flower, write the project you're working on. Use each petal to create stages along your cycle, such as who you need to connect with, what is your first step, and what else you need to grow your idea from seed to flower. Look at this as ambition in motion, as a way of tracking one cycle of your ambitious purpose. Draw as many flowers as you desire to help inspire your projects or track how they're going and what you need to complete each of them.

To wrap up this part of the book, look back through your journal at the designs you've worked on. Finish any that still need to be worked through, update any that need refreshing, and get ready to utterly *bloom*.

Part Three
BLOOM AS YOUR PURPOSE

In this final section, I want to share with you all the daily rituals and soulful processes I use as an important part of living and expressing my purpose each day.

The chapters ahead are a guide to actualizing and sharing your purpose. This is where you bloom. This is how your petals unfurl according to the impetus of light within your being. Now that you've visualized your path and designed the elements, it's time to harness your courage, dare to fail, and live your wild-hearted purpose every day.

These techniques are meant to be personalized in *any* way you desire. Use all of them—or just the ones you resonate with—in ways that enliven your message, gifts, and service. Take these ideas and create with them through your own radical and inimitable energy.

Chapter 7

RITUALS OF ABUNDANCE

*"We trust in the Earth and the Sun and the Stars
and allow ourselves to be held.
We do nothing alone."*[15]
—Elen Elenna

When you curate the kind of morning ritual that involves welcome and praise for the rising sun, rather than complaints or worries, you set yourself up to have a day full of possibility and abundance. Beginning with a high vibration draws everything good into your realm.

When you complete each day under the stars in gratitude for all you've received, you become more in tune with the flow of nature and the blessings of the earth.

When you rise into the dawn of a creative project, new job, or inspiring collaboration with a positive mindset and grateful heart, you realize your dream with open arms.

Holding gently on to your vision, looking hopefully and confidently to your design, you know when it's time to bloom. And with a smile, you begin.

---

15. Elen Elenna, *Silver Wheel: The Lost Teachings of the Deerskin Book* (London: Head of Zeus, 2016), 106.

WELCOME EACH DAWN WITH SELF-BELIEF

Living without attachments to the past (qualifications, achieve-
ments, career peaks) or expectations of the future (career bucket
list, detailed five-year plan, desired earnings) gives you the ability
to surrender to the kind of intuitive abundance and aligned opportunities that are meant for you. Create as many plans and lists as
you like, but remember ... life likes to surprise those who are open
to Spirit.

• JOURNEY •
Allowing the Next Version of You

Observe yourself sitting with your community, pondering how
intimately and lovingly you know them. You've learned about
yourself and received many important lessons from your Soul family. You've spread your wings so wide and free while you've been
in this space. Now your heart is calling you to another place. The
destination is unknown, but the urge to move on, which came to
you overnight in dreams and stars, is strong.

You hand over your practice to a local group of teachers. You
trade the belongings you don't need for food and traveling equip-
ment. You sit down with your beloved and explain that you need to
move to a new place; you're being animated from the drumming
of your ancient heart, and you cannot resist it for a moment. You
invite them along without any persuasion, knowing that they will
have heard the call or not; you cannot interfere with their course.
They decide to let you go for a short while, knowing they will see
you again somewhere magnificent soon. A bittersweet farewell is
shared, and you leave feeling love and gratitude.

As you walk away, you find yourself in a rocky clearing with
the sun beaming its rays all over you. You take off your pack and

kneel. With one hand on your chest and the other on your belly, you breathe the golden light into your whole being.

In every bone and cell of your body, you feel safe wherever you go. This wildhearted path you walk may be unmapped, but there are no accidents along this route of love.

A blessing falls from your lips and drops into the morning breeze:

> *May I feel the undeniable love of Great Spirit who*
> *lives and breathes within my Soul.*
> *May I be held by Mother Earth's embrace with*
> *every step.*
> *May I be guided by the plants and elements so that all*
> *my needs are met.*
> *May I be blessed by the animals and nature spirits*
> *who walk beside me.*
> *I devote my purpose to this path of Love.*
> *I am One with all.*
> *And so it is.*

Looking up, you see a python curled around a tree branch looking intently at you. Feeling the need to shed your old energy before your next adventure, you draw an imaginary arch over the clearing in front of you. You set an intention for transformation and allow your finger to intuitively draw lines and shapes within the arch. It feels like sacred geometry weaving a web in a doorway for you to walk through.

As you step through the energetic entrance, you allow any dense residue to fall behind you and be transmuted with love by Mother Earth. You let go of all attachments from your community. You set yourself free to grow into the next version of you without expectations or pressure.

You keep walking, bare feet activated and ready to explore new lands, eyes wide with excitement, mind full of cherished memories, and a creative heart willing to start afresh.

BEGIN THE DAY WELL AND FOLLOW THE SUN

I have found within my own fluid connection to daily rituals an important practice I love to do each morning. When I wake up, no matter how early, how my body feels, how much sleep I've had, or what's going on in my life, I place my left hand on my belly and my right hand on my heart and breathe golden morning sunshine into my being. I expand the light of my own being and speak beautiful, positive, generous, healing, and calming words to myself.

I say this or something to this effect: "I am healing deeply in every cell. I love my body, my human vessel of love. I am a radiant being of luminous, endless light. I humbly follow my wise heart each day toward a life overflowing with abundance. I am strong and capable enough to handle all situations today. All I desire flows to me. I honor the land where I live. All is well."

I believe these words, I own them, I feel them, I let them alchemize any doubt, fear, or lack into a higher way of being. I've learned that days that begin with complaints about sleep or concerns about the day ahead take a lot more energy to maneuver through than the ones that begin with a blessed ritual of gratitude. I surrender the falsehoods, trivialities, pain, and illusions that aren't mine and focus on what *is* mine: my limitless, bounteous, ecstatic, and daring Soul.

At the dawn of each day, I recognize the opportunity to *begin the day well* and live in a positive vibration that develops momentum throughout the day as I hold the intentions close to my heart.

Throughout my life, there have been many dawns that have inevitably followed dark nights of the Soul. These dawns feel pristine, gleaming, and precious. Whenever I've hit the rocky bottom of a particularly uncomfortable valley of endings, trauma, illness, loss, grief, or other challenges, the rise back into the healing sunshine is always so sweet.

It's in these dawns, these gifts from our awakening Souls, when we are able to set an uplifting intention for the next stage of life.

Life isn't predictable, careers aren't linear, and our purpose isn't necessarily to hold steadfast onto one particular job or vocation unless that is what our hearts call us to do. Life is a series of evolutionary leaps that take us onto higher outlooks and more expansive perspectives of life. Each dawn calls us to review our life, work, relationships, habits, residence, and thoughts and, if necessary, make appropriate changes.

Our purpose is to follow the lead of our heart no matter what through the depths and vistas.

Knowing that our Soul is the same spark of Source energy that lives within everyone else, and yet it speaks uniquely through our heartspace, gives us the capacity to trust deeply in the wisdom that flows from here. Nothing is ever a mistake, and we are never journeying alone.

As you take your first conscious breath of each day, choose a ritual that weaves together mind, body, and spirit; gratitude, positivity, and joy; safety, wellness, and groundedness. Remind yourself of the blessing of new beginnings, so that as you create newness in your career and life, you'll walk in faith with each step as you *follow the sun* and are met with miracles and abundance.

· RITUAL ·

Intuitive Morning Body Connection

Create a morning ritual that connects you to your physical body, your energetic heart, your infinite spirit, and your luminous mind.

Start each day in any way that feels loving and reverent. Try the ideas outlined below if you're not sure where to start, then keep at the ritual every day until a change feels necessary, or create your own whenever you desire.

- Mirror reflection. Place one hand on your heart. Look at your uniquely magnificent eyes in the mirror and tell yourself how radiant, magical, worthy, adored, divine, and important you are. Use your own words as they flow from your heart. Keep looking at yourself as you receive each compliment. It may be uncomfortable at first; keep connecting in gradually longer periods until you are relaxed and look forward to the ritual each morning. If you resist telling yourself anything positive, notice where you hold resistance and breathe through it.

- Daily loving affirmations. In the first moment of each day, before your eyes open, place your hands on your body wherever they feel soothing (hips, belly, heart, and shoulders are relaxing points on your body) and say gently positive affirmations to yourself—internally or out loud. Your hands will help embody the energy as the words move through you, while a genuine mindset will accept the words as real. Speak to yourself in the first person—*I* or *me*—and use positive words. Keep to the same affirmations each morning to build up their power, or intuitively tune in to what you need each day and speak from your heart.[16]

- Rising sun breathwork. During your morning routine, take a moment to renew your lifeforce with morning light. Find a place in nature or a space in your home with a sunlit view or poster of sunny nature and sit cross-legged, facing east if you can, on a cushion if you need it. Place your hands in prayer position or overlapping on your heart and close your eyes. If you can't see the morning sun pouring gently through your eyelids, imagine it is doing so. Welcome the light into your being and breathe deeply and naturally into your belly and lungs. Let the breath be long and pause at the end of each in-breath and out-breath for as long as is comfortable. Imagine the breath renewing your lifeforce and the light revitalizing your every cell. Feel whole, healed, and well. After five to ten minutes of this practice, place your hands in prayer position at your third eye and bow to the sun, acknowledging its important role in your physical, mental, emotional, and spiritual health.

While I enjoy regular rituals, I'm also innately attuned to the fresh energy of the cosmos and the unique needs of my body each day. As I soak up the sun's daily rise, I open to the codes of light from the sun, which feel different each day. As I say daily affirmations in bed or in front of the mirror, I'm aware of the words and sensations I'm strongly drawn to in that moment. You may feel the power and depth of repetitive actions and words, or you may

16. You can access a range of my published affirmations at krisfranken.com /daily-affirmations.

be more fluid with the timing and content of your ceremony. No matter how often or in what ways you show up, honor yourself.

CALL ON YOUR SOUL'S WILD EXPANSE

When we learn to listen to what is calling to us in the present moment, we become mindfully powerful cocreators with all of life. It takes patience to live and create this way, to honor what is in front of us rather than leaning into the past or predicting the future. Everything you need is within you *now*.

· JOURNEY ·
Hearing and Heeding the Call

You're now at the beginning of a whole new, unpredictable adventure. Witness this fresh start with awe, walking through wetlands along a scenic salt marsh. At a gentle curve, you find a pink-and-white conch shell. Curious at how far this shell must have drifted from the ocean, you find a place to rest and listen to the hum within it.

As you lie in the long grass with the shell next to your ear and your bare feet in the still salt water, you hear the air swirling through the hollows of the shell's cavern. Between the swishes, you make out a journey of a creature who followed nature's course through estuaries, along the subtle pull of the inner shoreline, toward a place it longed for without reason.

You smile a wide smile of heartfelt recognition. This is your journey, too. And although the creature has long left the protective home of its shell behind, its spirit is delighted to be connecting with you at this intersection of your journey.

The shell is quiet for a moment, then it asks you to whisper back into its smooth recesses. You close your eyes and connect to your animated lifeforce. You set an intention for the next part of your journey, then whisper it into the shell ... words of trusting the process, serving those in need of your medicine, and opening to receive enough abundance so you can create a home where you can call back your beloved.

You sleep in this serene place for a while, the shell resting on your heartspace. When you wake, you rise and, with permission, place the shell into your bag as you feel you'll need its medicine for a little while longer.

You walk toward more solid ground, hearing the call of a new community, a higher purpose, a deeper connection to the gifts of purpose that are evolving within you.

EXPANDING TIME IN A MOMENT

There's a moment I've found to be often overlooked but palpably potent when it comes to living out my dreams. It's the full breath just before action, before the connection is made, the email sent, the parcel delivered, the launch of a creation.

It's an opportunity to tune way, way down deep into the hollow womb of creation and call on all you know and all you need. It's the moment between being ready to go and walking out the door, and it may be needed at any stage of the creative process.

Expanding time in a moment.

Rushing never created anything beautiful in my life. For me, rushing is a lack of focus, an insecure hurry, and a guaranteed way to run past the inner heartsong. Rushing lacks trust and pushes against the intrinsic flow and cycles of life.

One simple, conscious, and deep breath calls me back into my presence, asks me to trust in the divinely guided process, to remember why I began this journey and who it's for.

In this breath is my full presence. And in my presence, I can access my Soul's wise expanse. This is how I bloom.

We cannot give all the time without breathing and opening to receive. We cannot go from one stage of our purpose to another without a quiet moment of reflection and gratitude, time to process what has been and proceed toward what shall be with a clear mind and open heart.

During sixteen years of writing magazine articles, I learned that the best gift I could give each article—if I was to be truly happy with it—was a day of rest before I edited it one last time and sent it off. I found that if I wrote the article right up to the deadline, then sent it in without pause, I inevitably felt frustrated at the incompleteness of the published article.

Tending to my breath before important action changed my level of fulfillment greatly.

It's the same with all my creations. The breath is never a waste of time—it's the opposite; it *expands* time. In the overall picture of creativity, it saves time, energy, and frustration.

When the breath is utilized to also surrender attachment to the creation process, then the next step—whether that's editing, sending, launching, sharing, opening, or introducing—will feel coherent and easy.

Learn to be still before you begin, to *expand time in a moment.* Now that your design is complete—but always available for editing and upleveling—give yourself a moment of presence to sit within the space of readiness. Savor this moment, relish the work you've done so far, take a deep breath, and prepare to shine every color of your rainbow.

· PRACTICE ·
Expansive Pause Soul Prompts

Tune in to your purpose or perhaps something you're ready to create, be, or share. Take out your notepad and answer these questions.

- Where in your life are you too busy? How are you being called to pause and pull your energy back into soft, patient beingness? How will you make space to breathe and what will you do to sink yourself fully into the mindful moment?

- How does it feel to allow stillness into your day? Can you create a daily ritual of stillness, either through meditation, sitting in nature, or an afternoon nap? Try sitting somewhere cozy for ten minutes in the morning or evening. Connect your natural breath with the rising sun or glistening stars, without needing to do anything else but allow your lifeforce to flow.

- Write about trusting in this process. Do you trust that in the slow, easeful moments of your day you aren't wasting time? Do you feel able to deepen your purpose and be more creative, conscious, and clear when you step back into the flow of your day? Do you trust that your body is better for resting?

Beam Your Luminous Presence

When we focus solely on the biggest dreams of our lives, we can become overwhelmed with how huge the mountains of creation seem. When we instead bring our focus to our presence each day, we can fulfill our smaller dreams and serve others in a more mindful way. It's these smaller dreams that join to create a life of monumental fulfillment and joy.

· Journey ·
Serendipitous Moments of Reflection

Continuing on this mythical path, you sense a deepening trust in this expanse of nature. You feel so astonishingly at home and on purpose even in the middle of nowhere doing nothing in particular except being *all* of who you are.

The freedom you are experiencing is beyond what you thought you were capable of. You realize you are truly free because you have been completely honest about who you are and what you want in life, not hooked into other people's paths or desires.

In the weeks you spend walking along the coast to find a seaside community, you're enchanted by many creatures on land and in water. The elements reflect your inner state of limitless liberation. Serendipitous moments come to you regularly; rainbows and butterflies are your constant companions. And when you fall over, sprain your ankle, and receive a small spider bite, help comes immediately, humor quickly follows, and you heal swiftly.

During an afternoon swim in late fall, you see movement in the deeper waters. Out of the oceanic blue, a dolphin swims alongside you, singing with you and inviting you to play. Together you dip and dive, nudging each other gently as you follow the current.

Soon the dolphin retreats to their pod, and you feel the lingering, nurturing energy of family and community. You sense your community is almost in reach.

With the ebb and flow of the dolphin's medicine still swirling in your being, you make your way inland slightly, sweeping around small towns and shops. You can see how easy it would be to slip into a town or city and remain unknown for a while. But your heart knows it thrives in connection with others and the earth.

You continue north, taking faithful steps until eventually you see a circle of tents. Beaming with joy, your medicine and love overflowing, you are welcomed into the community.

That night as you connect with a Soul brother around a fire, you notice a pendant on his necklace sparkling in the flame light. It catches your eye again and again until you look closer. You laugh when you notice the curves of a polished dolphin, smiling at you from beyond, acknowledging you for following your heart all the way home.

Wayward Heart, Wildest Dreams

I never found a way to fit in. I've always felt like a solitary, stubborn, wayward freesia blooming in the middle of a perfect lawn: persistently out of place, yet somehow happy just being me.

Growing up in the church, I didn't feel completely at ease or at home, though I made much-loved friends. In my family I was the stubborn, rebellious one. At university, while I came alive studying a wide range of captivating subjects, I felt like I was the only one confused about where I was headed in life.

When it came to my career, it was always the same: I would find the job I wanted, get promoted too quickly for my capabilities or experience, and swiftly feel like an incapable and insecure manager who tried a little too hard to befriend others. Each job was deeply rewarding and taking me where I needed to go, but I was stretched too far and found it difficult to say no. Burnout and panic attacks ensued while chronic anxiety kept me forever on edge.

I never wanted the easy route, never yearned for the premade career selection, never could follow in the steps of another. I was called selfish, stubborn, willful, lazy, and distracted. I drank too much alcohol to numb the frustration at the lack of satisfaction and peace in my life. And yet, I worked hard. Wherever I went, even if it wasn't the perfect job, I was all in.

I changed jobs according to the whims of my heart (while honoring my responsibilities), not the suggestions of others. Slowly, these whims became whispers, which turned into solid, loving nudges from within. Shortly after I was retrenched from the last job I ever had working for someone else (as a beauty and health editor on a magazine), I found myself with a hot cup of tea, all alone with a window full of trees, no one to direct me or schedule my day, no clear path before me, and no map to drop a pin on. Only a deeply exciting blog, a stack of freelance articles to write, and a longing to create a book. I finally felt free to bask in the radiance of my calling. It felt wild, unpredictable, and *mine*. This wayward freesia was finally in her element.

It's no coincidence that this career highlight happened at the same time I discovered friends who felt like fellow freesias, rituals that seemed ancient and true, and hobbies that lit me up with unlimited joy from the inside out. This was also the time when I discovered and accepted who I was through curious consideration, began to heal my anxiety and collection of traumas, and faithfully surrendered to my heart.

While diving into the endless pools of self-exploration, I learned why I'm here on earth at this time: to empower others, to guide them back onto the way of their wise hearts. This influential understanding came once I healed my deepest scars enough to feel safe and grounded in life. This groundedness finally anchored me into the present moment, which is where I found my dream calling and most magnificent friendships, clients, and opportunities.

It's through the sublime present moment that we're able to access the whole spectrum of insight within in the multidimensional universe. When we show up each day, curious and centered, we are shown all we need to know for the day ahead. We may get glimpses of our future, but our energy expands the most when we are fully alive in our raw state, connected to nature, in the timeless now.

I don't look back at the life before this moment as being anything other than perfect. It all had a reason, a lesson, a treasure to collect on my path. Looking back, I can see how I was navigating life according to my heart, even if it was edgy, messy, and challenging. I can see that I walked my purpose like a free Soul travels the land: according to ley lines and seasons, in communion with stars and the moon, without regard for maps or rules, and in alignment with love. No matter how thick the grass or how dry the dirt, I was that one unyielding freesia, pushing her way up toward the sunshine, ready to beam my luminous presence.

It turns out, I never really wanted to fit in. I only ever wanted to live out my *wayward heart's wildest dreams.*

· PRACTICE ·
Luminous Soul Prompts

It's natural for humans to want to fit in with their communities— to be with a group of people who are similar to us in many ways, people to have endless conversations with, people who support and appreciate our unique ways.

Problems arise when we conform to a group that isn't open-minded or like-hearted, or when we try to receive approval from those who don't genuinely appreciate us. A vacuous feeling sinks in when we seek to fit in with the "world," celebrities, or trends driven by the media. Unsettling confusion grows within us when we mistake online connections for real-life community. There's no substitute for grassroots love, communion, and support.

Can you remember a time when you stepped out on your own and did something your heart had been calling you to do, but was a surprise to other people? Consider this moment in your life. Call in to your memory as many details as you can and hold them with love while you answer the following questions in your journal.

- What did you do that seemed rebellious to yourself or others? What made it so defiant or unexpected? Take your time answering this; unpack the whole moment on paper for you to recall fully with gentleness.

- Why was your heart nudging you in that direction? In hindsight, what was so important about your brave move?

- What was the outcome? If it was positive, how has that shifted your life for the better? If it was negative, how was it an important lesson for you on your path? Did you connect with people who felt aligned with your energy because of what you did?

- Remembering this from a higher perspective, what would you like to say to your younger self about the importance of living free, brave, and heartfelt?

- How can you take the highlights of this event and apply what you learned to the challenges or opportunities you currently face? What would your younger self say to you now?

Learning to be sovereign and Soul-driven in your life will bring you closer to those who have similar interests and spark an energy that fuels your adventurous desires. These people will desire harmony but never demand conformity (and if they do, it's a sign that the group is out of balance with its collective heart and purposeful mission); rather, they will spur you and your holy rebellion on to be the wildest version of you.

Chapter 8

SYNC WITH CYCLES
AND FLOW

*"You will know when you are in harmony with the Universe,
because you will be in harmony with your spirit."*[17]
—SARAH MCLEOD

There's a flow that's intrinsic to your being, a flow that is naturally in sync with your inner cycles and the seasons around you. It doesn't need external creation or force to come to life; it's a simple, quiet movement that is already a living part of you.

Every step you take that goes against this inner fluidity feels unnatural, uncomfortable. It feels like putting on someone else's shoes or wearing a jacket that's too small. And yet, we so often get used to discomfort for the sake of pleasing others, conforming, valuing the empty hustle, or because we haven't been in touch with our lifeforce before.

The flow isn't only within us, it's between us and nature, us and other people, us and *life itself*. This chapter is about tuning in to this flow, feeling it fully, and honoring it. To reconnect with your inner nature is to reconnect with the vital nature of community and earth.

---

17. Sarah McLeod, *Spirit Guidance: Vision Weaving with Healing Energy* (Schenectady, NY: Citrine Publishing, 2020), 202.

SYMBIOTIC SUPPORT AND
SERVICE TO OTHERS

We know ourselves deeper in the reflection of others. We know our purpose so much greater when it is given to others. The more we give away our gifts, the more we receive abundance, satisfaction, and a pleasure that comes from serving community.

· JOURNEY ·
Just Like the Trees

See yourself spending the day in nature, foraging for a variety of native berries and healing mushrooms. You come across a family of tall, ancient, and strong trees, soothing to look at, promising shade and an opportunity to replenish your inner energy source. Your body is feeling sore, lethargic, and tender.

You sit up against one of these beautiful oaks with your back firm against the bark. You breathe in a long, deep, nourishing breath and sigh out a spacious sigh. The deeper you breathe, the more your head and heart expand. The louder you sigh, the less of a weight you carry in your body. Slowly, you curl up at the feet of a tree, roots hugging you, leaves filtering the heat of the late fall sun.

Looking around you, you notice you're in the middle of a circle of trees. You feel safe and supported. In this cocoon, you hear the echo of your breath and your sighs from deep within the supple, wooden hearts of these trees. Each breath reciprocated, each sigh repeated. The rhythm of this exchange lulls you into a long and longed-for afternoon nap.

As you doze, you dream of climbing into the center of the largest tree. As you clamber inside and your eyes adjust to the darkness, you notice light streaming from the deep pulse of earth through the roots. It fills you and the trunk all around you, then escalates up into the leaf-lined antennae, finally joining the cosmos of stars.

In your vision, you witness your heart, your loving presence, activated by this movement of light within the tree. You see and feel the symbiotic exchange of life, like an infinity symbol between humans and trees, between all life-forms.

You wake and remember ... *we are just like the trees*, like all beings of earth: energetic transmitters and receivers of light and love.

Symbiotic Momentum within Community

This uncertain and wondrous life isn't meant to be a lonely ride. The whole reason for purpose is what you bring to and receive from another. You'll inevitably be challenged, uplifted, strengthened, and soothed as you create with and serve the needs of others, and that's the point.

We *all* need community. Not just as a web of support and safety, but, importantly, as an avenue for the greatest service of our life's purpose. We need support and safety for us to survive; we need to give and receive of our gifts and energy for us to thrive.

This is *symbiotic momentum within community.*

When you channel your energy to serve your community from the deepest reaches of your heart and highest purpose of your Soul, you immediately enter into a symbiotic relationship with them. This goes beyond receiving financial abundance, though money is an important part of a purposeful life. As you reach out to support another, you will feel full of loving satisfaction. When you share your gifts with others, you will receive the gift of their appreciation. In honoring your role of service in your community—as important as all other roles—you will anchor your Soul's ancient wisdom into this life. Though not all interactions will be equally beneficial or genuine, we need to remain mindful of our own intentions and trust that overall there is a greater plan working in our favor.

In welcoming the gifts, wisdom, love, support, and treasures from others in your community who are living their highest purpose, you give to them a deeper connection to their purpose, intention, and truth. Like trees and humans keep each other alive, we genuinely need each other to breathe inspiration and creativity into our lives.

The symbiotic movement of energy between all of us is extraordinary. At times you may notice you're unconsciously blocking the flow by not receiving openly or not giving of yourself freely. When you notice a block, you may sense a disconnection from those around you or your own spirit. Come home to yourself and try the three processes listed below to open yourself to cascading energy flow.

When you become conscious and trusting of the those around you, you become one with divine flow and the most natural state of being. As the late and inimitable Guru Jagat wrote in her book *Invincible Living* about discovering destinies and higher frequencies, "When you don't know why you're here, you just have one mandate and it's actually quite simple! In every moment of every day, you create more prayer, more *love,* and more genuine interaction between human beings, and you see where that takes you. This energy will open up the chambers of your destiny and, ultimately, the powerfully magnetic energy of your heart."[18]

---

18. Guru Jagat, *Invincible Living: The Power of Yoga, the Energy of Breath, and Other Tools for a Radiant Life* (San Francisco, CA: HarperCollins, 2017), 246.

· Ritual ·
Expansive State of Flow

Connect with these three processes regularly and take note of how your life expands to be more in flow with the Universe.

- **Abundance Tree.** Sit in a quiet and comfortable space where you won't be disturbed. Breathe deeply in and out through your nose until you notice a calming relaxation sweep through your being. Imagine you are just like a tree, with deep roots and expansive branches of light that reach the sunshine. Feel your strong energetic roots connecting deeply into the earth. Feel or see yourself drawing on Gaia's nourishing light, up through your roots and the trunk of your body, then imagine it spreading out into the branches and leaves above your head. Now notice the light of the sun shining onto each leaf and branch, pouring its luminescence all the way down into your roots. Visualize this tree glowing fully with the abundance of light that is always available to you. Feel your heart open to the whole Universe; let it expand and expand until you are awash with bliss. Let the light within unlock a new access to financial wealth, soulful community, creative ideas, blissful health, good health, and clear intuition. Know with your whole being that you are taken care of in every moment by the Universe. Take about twenty minutes to meditate on your inner abundance tree each day for a week or two and notice how life flows more magically.

- **Complete Acceptance Ritual.** Take this mantra and say it out loud or silently to yourself whenever you are given a gift. Gifts come in a wide variety of bounty—the gift can be a compliment, a kind comment on social media, a piece of fruit from a tree in your yard, a song from a bird, a healing from a practitioner, a hug from a loved one, a shell from the beach, a payment from a client, or a message from your nature guides. Say this: "I receive with ease this gift from life, and I open to receive all blessings that are meant for me. I am grateful to be in the flow of abundance. And so it is."

- **Journal from Love.** When you become conscious of any blocks in your life to giving or receiving abundance, take out your journal and write what you believe to be the problem. If you don't know clearly, try seeing the block from a higher perspective. When you find the root—whether it's a word, sentence, belief, or idea—ask yourself, "What would Love do?" and write the answer as though the highest form of energy—Love—is giving you advice straight through your heart.

FLOW WITH THE CYCLES OF LIFE

Many of us live in cultures that don't honor who or what is dying, be it an animal, a human life, or the end of a job, relationship, or era. All too often we move on quickly, evading the heaviness of grief, consumed with aliveness, ready for the next big adventure, hopeful for everlasting happiness. But death is a portal into another realm, and when we honor each death as though the dying is important and needs space in which to decompose completely, we come to life with a deeper reverence and humility than ever before.

· JOURNEY ·
Breathtaking Mountain Healing

Feel what it would be like after sleeping on and off during the fall season for what feels like a month or two. You had just found a beautiful community to join when your body fell into an unexpectedly long spell of slow living. One day, you wake with the urge to climb. Your once fatigued body feels stronger; the rest has been a salve for your bones, muscles, thoughts, and spirit.

All this time you wondered what would cause your energy to deflate so deeply that you could barely sense your natural force of light and life. Downhearted and dispirited, you chose rest, knowing that resisting and relenting against your body would cause far more pain.

Frustration turned to peace; struggle, to surrender. The softness expanded you in unforeseen ways, and you received from your community an endless supply of nourishment, from your lengthy sleep many prescient dreams, and from the Universe an array of magic. You were held in your healing space until every part of you in all time, space, and dimensions was whole.

Placing your feet on the ground, you feel a surge of lifeforce from Gaia. Raising your arms in the air, you give thanks to the greater divinity watching over you. Layering your hands on your heart, you feel the love within you. You are ready to move, climb, and grow.

As your legs gratefully follow the softest grass and your glowing eyes track the brightest star, the last one to sleep, the unfolding of your next adventure begins. In the depth of your reprieve, you broke the spell of busy-ness and weaved a new story together of patience and wonder. And now, in your tender power and mindful presence,

you feel each breath with reverence while moving in sweet appreciation of the evolution of consciousness within.

Your love of mountains has always been resolute, but only
recently have you connected heart-to-heart with them. The rapture, healing, and admiration are mutual.

On this morning, the mountain seems to come to you as you
flow toward it. With gleeful anticipation, you step onto the first
rock, then the next as you climb to the place where you cross over.
As the air thins slightly and your lungs expand, your trust grows
as deep as you go high. Love takes you upward into the clouds of
transformation.

Faithful feet and hopeful hands kiss each rock, and loving eyes
greet each unseen nature being along the way. Animals take time
to revel in your unique presence; they marvel at your rainbow
aura, a grand fusion of colors from your deep inner healing work.

Soon a crossing appears just underneath the majestic peak
where you're able to glimpse trees and waterways from the highest
view. Without the rest period, you may never have met with this
mountain with such phenomenal resolution. Here you stand, taking in a breathtaking view above the clouds, looking across on all
that awaits you.

Your heart hums as though it's resonating with the Mother;
you hum out loud as though She is reverberating through you.
Soon an eagle comes near you and sits on a rock. He looks you in
the eye and transmits a message of light to you. The hum of your
heart becomes more ecstatic, your spine straightens, and you feel
energetic wings forming and swelling on your back. The eagle flies
away, the exchange complete.

As you take in this blissful perspective with a wiser, more heightened awareness through the eyes of eagles, you see a cloud gliding

toward you. This cloud is not made of usual swells of raindrops—it's made of stardust, and it glimmers electrically in the afternoon sun.

The cloud approaches you as though it was sent for you. You stand, palms facing out, eyes closed. The cloud moves around and through you, and with your next breath, you plunge through a portal of mountain air and higher-dimensional light beams. Your whole being shivers with bliss.

Elated, you move gently halfway down the mountain to rest and ponder this incredible day. This morning you were healing, and now you're completely transformed, as though a part of you died on top of the mountain and rebirthed into a new being. Your inner vision is sharp like an eagle's, your Soul medicine has been refreshed by a cloud of light, and the mountain has infused your heart with majestic love.

SACRED CYCLES OF LIFE

Throughout your Soul's life, you will inevitably move through cycles of birth, life, death, and afterlife many times. Within your own life, this particular incarnation, you will experience it continually.

Within each life, this cycle can be both literal and metaphorical. It helps us understand the cyclical nature of all creation. "Birth" is the beginning of all newness in your life, such as jobs, creativity, relationships, and children. "Life" is the aliveness that comes when the existence of a creation is sustained for some time. "Death" is the end of a chapter in your life. It can also mean the physical death of a loved one where the phase of grief honors the loss of their life. "Afterlife," or "transcendence," comes after death, for death is never truly the end, only the pause before a new beginning. Afterlife is often the stage of awakening to a higher understanding at the end of a cycle through transcendence, meaning "moving beyond."

This is the *sacred cycle of life*.

Many fear this natural and perfect cycle because they don't understand the necessity of loss and death as a natural part of life. They fear losing a job, ending a relationship, moving to a new area, wrapping up a creative project, and especially, death itself.

When a tree dies, we use the wood to keep warm, to preserve our lives, or to build buildings in which to live and love. When wildflowers die, they spread their seeds all over the ground, ready for the next season of renewal. The energy of a being—tree, flower, human, or other—never disappears completely. There is no complete death because energy cannot die; it is transmuted into something else, a living legacy of its sentient existence.

There is no death of the true self.

Within the period of life, we have our own cycles that keep us growing, learning, resting, awakening, reaching a higher purpose. Feeling fully alive and set to an "on" position is exhilarating for a while before it becomes exhausting. There need to be ebbs and flows within the life cycle for balance to be achieved.

Rest is an essential part of life. It allows deep healing to occur on every level. When we take time to slow our pace to heal and honor what is dying, we also pull back from busy-ness, the rush of other people's energies, and the attentive work that calls to us daily. Inside this soft cocoon, we allow ourselves to wholly let go. It is here, in the safety of surrender, where we hear what has been spoken for so long, but not heard.

In the silence, we hear the truth of living wild and loving service, of devoted work and pleasureful play, of intimate relationships and close family, of unmet needs and unwanted desires, of obsolete ways and misaligned plans.

We need not wait until we are sick to hear what is flowing from our hearts. We can create space to set a fresh intention each month, to give birth to a new day with a glowing candle, to allow our outdated identity a quiet death in a sacred space, and to transcend our mind within the silence of breath. We can sell or give many of our possessions away, live simply for a while. Or just set aside time to rest in peace while we're still alive.

Out of devotion to surrender, we find we are able to hear the nudges, witness the knowing, feel the direction of new life awakening.

In devotion to rest, we restore our being and allow the softness and strength of our being to rejuvenate. We see life differently and are able to balance the high energy of service with the softer energies that beckon us.

We move more purposefully in every way. We lose interest in trivial aspects of life and crave a deeper meaning. Resting is not a divergence of our purpose, but an opening to the greater gifts of it.

After the births of my two beautiful children, I experienced the birth of myself as a mom, a new life of profound expansion, the death of an outdated version of myself, and rebirth into a higher state of health, perspective, and purpose. The death was brutal; there was so much I needed to let go of. Like many of my generation, I incarnated at this time to heal ancestral wounds and past-life karma so that humanity can move into a new age with a refreshed slate. It's a lot to take on, being the bridge between ages. I'm grateful my children were the catalyst for much of that healing.

I healed lifelong anxiety, postnatal depression, alcohol obsession, severe past-life wounding, bone-deep anger, childhood trauma, unfathomable unworthiness, and the cutting limits I had placed on myself. With every healing, with every experience of transcendence, came a clearer vision, a deeper truth, and awareness of more unconditional love than ever before.

Eleven years after my firstborn arrived earthside, we moved into the rainforest. The months that followed our move were a profound life/death initiation. I stepped onto the highest level of empowered purpose when I hosted my first retreat near Mount Warning four weeks after we moved into our home. The ridges that extend from Mount Warning—known as *Wollumbin* to the local Indigenous people, meaning "cloud catcher"—meet with the ridges and valleys around my new home. Being so close to this incredible mountain was overwhelmingly invigorating, and the work and healing the women did together on retreat was life-changing.

Experiencing my first natural disaster less than a week after I returned home from the retreat felt traumatic, shattering, extraordinary. The rain that poured from the sky for five days and nights was so intense, I felt like I went through the toughest experience of my life. Physically, mentally, emotionally, and spiritually, I was challenged to the core. All around me were flooded homes, landslides, and sinkholes; I lost my emotional footing, and it took months to heal from the experience.

If my retreat was the birth of a new level of being, then the flood was a death of all the old ways that no longer served my highest purpose; it gave me a stronger focus on my immediate and beloved community and their needs. It showed me what needed to be healed from my past (especially ancient lives) to be reborn into a more spacious, honest, purposeful being in this new age.

I wasn't prepared for the rebirth that was to come only three weeks after the flood.

My husband and I invited two close friends to stay on our property to help with the magnificently wild yet overwhelming garden. They've become like family; such is the power of intentional community.

Tash was pregnant when she moved in and was looking forward to a peaceful birth in the luscious forest, preferably by the creek or in their bell tent. Repeatedly I received a vision of her birthing in our large bathtub, so occasionally I would mention to her that if she needed our bath during the birth, I would make it happen.

On a stunning Thursday morning, I woke to the echoing sounds of Tash roaring through the valley. I went to gently check in on her. Her tent was too hot, the creek was too cold, and her birth pool had a leak in it. My husband cleared the kids out of the house, I filled the bath and surrounded it with crystals and candles, called in the Ancestors, the Goddess, and the Ancient Ones, and Tash gratefully sank her exhausted, laboring body into the warm rainwater. Her partner held her in the most powerful force of love for the next four hours until her son was born; I did what I could to empower, protect, and guide her. I experienced every kind of emotion and sat with thoughts of death, injury, responsibility, doubt, and angst. I moved through a portal of accelerated purpose as a precious boy descended through his own birth portal in my bathtub.

The moment he began to cry, Tash's partner and I hugged, cried, and laughed together. I have never experienced that level of physically and emotionally activated bliss in my life. The elation and joy that poured through me was indescribable.

This was the rebirth of my purpose in the *sacred cycle of my life.*

With every cycle in your life, you'll come closer to your purpose. Birth will show you how strong, creative, and brave you are. Life will bring you fully into the light of day and allow you to share your luminescence. Death will bring many gifts, especially healing and the closure of what isn't meant for you anymore. Afterlife will take you to a higher realm for rebirth, a pause to reconcile the life that was and dream in the next incarnation of your calling.

There will be times when you'll be in some or all the stages of birth, life, death, and rebirth at the same time. You may be ending a relationship while birthing a new creative project. You might be loving a perpetual side hustle while swimming through the afterlife of grief from the death of a beloved pet, friend, lover, partner, or family member.

Don't be afraid of endings or hesitant to walk away from what isn't for you. And remember to be grateful for all that is alive within and around you. In the death of the old, you're given a chance to clear the slate, rest, open to a higher vision, redesign a more expansive plan, and step fully into a rebirth process with renewed strength and clarity.

· PRACTICE ·
Cycles of Life Soul Prompts

These journal prompts will help you understand better how your purpose is flowing perfectly through the cycles of life. Take out your journal and divide a page into four sections.

1. Give one section the header "Birth" and write down all aspects of your career, jobs, purpose, hobbies, and interests that are currently being birthed. All newness, all fresh ideas, everything you've just started, thought of, dreamed of, or explored.

2. Name your next section "Life" and write down what is in full bloom. All aspects of your purpose that are expanded into their fullness and radiating life. All parts of your career that are having their day in the sun.

3. Give another section the header "Death" and note everything that is coming to an end, either naturally or by your decision. All endings, what you're ready to

let go of, everything in its last act, all that you need closure from. Take time to acknowledge what you've received from what has ended, as well as the relief, grief, or spaciousness that may be present.

4. Give the final section the header "Afterlife" and note what has come from all that has died or completed its cycle. Eventually this may become something ready to be born anew. All opportunities that came to you when you completed something else, clarity that arrived when you reached a fresh attitude or approach, and all you're transcending in the name of goodness and love.

5. Now look at each section and see if anything is about to move. Can you detect a shift in the energy of anything you've noted? If so, simply draw an arrow, indicating that something is about to evolve into its next phase.

Give thanks for the cycles of life. When you know there is no true death, you will never fear it.

CREATE YOUR OWN DIVINE RHYTHM

We all have our own rhythm within the pulse of our being that drives the cadence of our creations. Some say this comes from watching our parents, others point to the stars we were born under, while many say it's simply our own intuitive way. The most powerful insight I've been gifted around my own brisk pace is knowing my birth imprint. The way I was born into this life can be seen in virtually all my creative processes. I'll share it with you shortly so you can understand your own.

· JOURNEY ·
Connected to a Greater Spirit

Continuing on the next phase of this visualization, see yourself immersed in this same community who held you while you rested. One auspicious day, you're all visited by a local animal healer, connected to the heart of Gaia and all Her creatures. People gather around them as they recount stories of animal connection and perception. They inspire and delight the whole community around the fire with stories of how they've been visited by the spirits of animals that have died in their care, and they speak of miraculous healing in birds, mammals, reptiles, and insects. They call in the spirit of Oneness with all living beings, and everyone feels this as lightness and awe. You feel overjoyed from their sharing, more connected to the voices and spirits that live with you on this sacred land.

As they are about to leave, they notice your overabundance of fruit from the many trees you grow together. They offer to trade a few animal skins—from beloved animals they have rescued, nurtured, and held through death—for a few boxes of fresh and dried fruit. You come together in a council to consider what you will use these skins for. Someone suggests they be used for shoes, another says drums and rattles, as your instruments are not as plentiful as you'd all like. Together you agree to accept the trade and begin your plan of lovingly creating drums and rattles.

When your visitor leaves, gratefully taking boxes of food to their own community, you meet with each other to bless and soak the hides of beloved goats and deer. Some members of the community set off to find fallen logs to make the drum frames and rattle handles. As these are being created, you cut the hides and prepare them for their rebirth.

When the circular frames are complete, a few of you take them with the hides to a sacred space on the land for creation. With bees and dragonfly visitors the only sound throughout the process, you each tend to your Shamanic creations.

When your drum is complete, you rest it in a warm, shady place to dry. You gather with the rest of the drum creators and notice that while some finished long before you, others are taking their time. You take the rest of your hide to another group for them to make rattles with.

As you sip an herbal tea, you revel in a day spent moving at your own pace and the emotions that have been lovingly felt through the process. You sit quietly with the others; as a group, you have woven together a deeply moving experience that leaves you feeling reflective, tranquil, and forever connected to the loving spirit of the animals.

CREATIVE BIRTH IMPRINTS

I've always been a fast worker. A little too fast, in fact.

I genuinely expect everything I create to happen quickly and perfectly. I've never felt this was bad or good, and I never felt too much pride or shame around it—I just knew it as my style. Without being conscious about the reasons behind this process in my creative life, I just happily showed up, made things happen in a whirlwind, tried to be as close to perfect as possible, and was done before most others (if there were others around).

When I catch a glimpse of what I want to make in a vision—whether it's oracle cards, a book, a retreat, women's circles, or an offering with clients—I'm usually in a rush to get it made. I love honoring the moment with as much momentum as possible. I tend to skim around the design stage, which I'm learning to deepen into (especially when writing a book), but I truly love the creation phase. It's where my joy is at.

Toward the end of a ten-month and deeply healing Shamanic circle in 2018, I was invited to attend a sacred retreat a few hours outside of Sydney, Australia. Since many of the women with whom I'd connected in the circle were going, I packed my bag and headed into the bush.

It was a drum making weekend with a women's mystery teacher called Anki, and it cracked my consciousness wide open around my innately creative process. Before we began making the drum with the hide of a goat, an animal with a naturally cheeky spirit, we sat in a circle and spoke about what we knew of our own birth. I was surprised because this isn't a subject I'd heard many women talk about; it was refreshing to hear so many stories of all kinds of births from all over our earth.

What we learned from Anki was that our births are our first creative process, and they imprint themselves on us during the first moment of our lives. It's a *creative birth imprint*. This was profound for me; it helped explain my creative process so uniquely and lovingly.

I was born in less than an hour at a hospital in Toronto, Canada. I came out fast, too fast if you ask my Mom, and that initial creative process has energetically etched itself into the way I work in all creative aspects of my life. From making dinner to planting flowers, writing poetry or designing a collage, I move with a lively pace, eager to be done. Even when I'm enjoying the process, I seem to enjoy the completion so much more.

The bright side is I move swiftly; the shadow side is I'm impatient. With a greater understanding of this intrinsic characteristic, I can balance the shadow and the light to meet in the middle. When I'm balanced, I'm able to listen to others, wait patiently for the right timing to land, and be compassionate toward any perceived imperfections.

We all have this impression within us. For those who, like me, were induced to be born, we may not appreciate others telling us what to do or when to do it. For others who, like my son, had a caesarean, they may not finish all their projects, or they may take their time with their creativity.

Your birth story tells a lot about your creative process, as does your astrology (my Virgo Rising has a lot to do with that perfectionist streak) and many other mediums and techniques. You don't need to concern yourself too much with *why* your creativity flows in the way it does—just accept your *creative birth imprint* as sacred, be open to healing the edges of it, and let the rest come from the heart.

If you're wondering, I was the second woman to finish my drum.

And it was gorgeous.

• PRACTICE •
Conscious Creation Soul Prompts

This practice—which I've adapted from my time with Anki with her blessing—will give you such powerful awareness of your personal process of creation. You'll begin to notice that how you cook dinner is the same as how you tend to the garden and how you knit a blanket. It's the same way you create a business, put your heart into products and services, and market yourself. It may be fast or slow, intricate or simple, rewarding or frustrating, but it's *your* process. Here's how you can understand your birth story to see how it's shaped your entire creative life.

Take out your notebook and answer the following questions as best as you can.

- Write all about your birth, calling on your mom or someone else who may remember it if you need to. If you don't have anyone to ask, go with what you know and intuit the rest.

- How many weeks' gestation was your mom at birth? Were you premature, "on time," or overdue? Looking back, how does that feel for you in relation to how you create?

- Were you born vaginally or by caesarean? Were there any tools used to help your birth, such as forceps? Were you induced? How has this imprinted on your creativity? Are you able to ask for help and receive it? Do you avoid interference? Are you able to initiate and complete creative projects?

- How long was the birth? If it was short or long, does this reflect in your creative journeys?

- Did your mom ask for any pain relief, medication, natural herbs, homeopathy, or an epidural? If so, can you sense a dimming down (maybe due to medication) or gentle amplifying (from natural remedies) of your energy through your processes?

- Were there any complications? What happened and what was the outcome?

- Were you with your mom after birth for long? Was there any separation? What was going on for you both during that time? Take your time with this question and see if you can compassionately unpack the answers to understand how these first moments have impacted your life within and beyond your creativity.

When you unwrap the precious details of your birth, you'll see how you can bring more consciousness into your life so you're in a balanced state—not rushing, stalling, procrastinating, or questioning the pace, just enjoying and expanding into the ride.

Chapter 9

BE GUIDED BY YOUR LIGHT

*"Look for Light with more intensity than ever ... If you look with
your Soul, you will keep finding Light everywhere."*[19]
—DANIELLE LAPORTE

Your true self is a being of astonishing light. You're a luminous,
expansive, incomparable expression of Source light, connected
through each lifetime to your one Soul, wrapped momentarily in a
human form, witnessing the light in all beings.

Recognizing that we are light—pure, holy intelligence—helps
us remember that it's not just our human self who is here on
earth, creating, loving, being, and exploring. Our human self is the
vessel, a miraculous form our light is able to radiate through.

When we feel into and call on our light to guide and direct
us along our path of purpose, we are intuitively tuning in to the
greatest, most accurate, and loving force available.

This light can be turned up or dimmed down by our daily
practices. That's what this chapter is about: consciously amplifying your Soul light and the energetic vibration within. When your

---

19.   Danielle LaPorte, *White Hot Truth: Clarity for Keeping It Real on Your Spiritual
      Path from One Seeker to Another* (Vancouver: Virtuonica, 2017), 132.

light is bright, those who need to find you will, and your truth will be lit from within.

HEAL TO RAISE YOUR VIBRATION

I've noticed a tendency in myself in the past to keep separate the various paths of life, as though they barely impact each other. I'll keep relationships in one parcel, my career in another, healing journeys separate, and anything else that's going on in its own neat and defined pocket. It helped me feel like I had more control over each aspect, although that was an illusion, and that's not how life works. From a greater perspective, *everything* is purpose. When I heal my body, my career shifts, abundance expands, relationships require adjustment, and whatever else is going on in my life is impacted as well. Over the last few years, I've learned that healing is the key to growth, ease, and magic along the path of my Soul's purpose.

· JOURNEY ·
Curative Love of the Ocean

Picture yourself on a leisurely fall afternoon, beating your drum on the sandy shore of the ocean, watching the full moon rise through the fading colors of the pastel sky.

Your rhythm is palpably, purposefully slow. Your heart calms, your breathing expands, and your whole body feels one with the pulse of Mama Gaia's heart.

While time on your own has given you an opportunity to explore the depths of heavier emotions tugging at your joy, it's also reminded you of how much you miss your beloved.

Grateful for this chance to go within, to gently explore your heart, you breathe deeply and surrender to the weight of the drum's rhythm syncing with each wave of the ocean.

You imagine the ocean as a goddess, green energy swirling from her heart across to yours, sparkling with golden glints, surrounding your whole being, infusing you with her ancient healing, and transmuting the heaviness into light, into love. Your whole being softens, expands, sighs with this curative experience.

Your heart energy expands until it's wrapped around your aura, swimming through the lights of your eyes, pulsating love within and without. You consciously direct your Soul's light, which radiates with Source energy, throughout your being, according to the direction of your spirit. Through organs and bones, awakening cells and lifeforce, along meridians and pathways, into the bloodstream and skin, it moves, powerfully, tenderly, shifting the energy higher, removing toxins, and allowing for greater health.

The drum guides the entire process, like your heart guides the flow of blood.

Giving thanks to your drum and Spirit for guiding you through this healing journey, you head into the ocean for a plunge. On your return, you're stunned to see your beloved has found you, called by the drum's ancient pulse, the moon's magnetic beams, and love's mysterious hand, and has brought a feast for dinner.

You embrace passionately. Your hearts rejoice. Your Souls shine with delight.

OPEN-HEARTED HEALING

Healing may not seem obvious or overly important within your purpose, but to me there is nothing more important than being radiantly healthy in my mind, body, and spirit for me to honor my calling each day. If I'm overwhelmed by low energy, poor sleep, ineffective concentration, physical pain, negative emotions, psychic attacks, or anxious thoughts, I may struggle to be of service or to clearly hear the direction of my heart.

By healing, I'm surrendering all that isn't mine to carry and creating space for more of my authentic truth to emanate.

It's through repeated *open-hearted healing* and surrender that I'm able to choose healthy habits, positive relationships, and career moves that honor and celebrate my unique self, rather than making choices to accentuate my ego's smallness, numb pain, repress trauma, or please others.

Healing has become *part* of my purpose, not just a separate *path*. The process of healing helps me become more aware of and connected to the abundant, symbiotic flow between myself and others. This flow is in its very essence purposeful; it accelerates my openness to receiving from others and from life itself, as well as allowing me to give of my whole, healed self.

My emotions indicate what needs tending to, surrendering, or appreciating. Understanding emotions from a spiritual and scientific perspective has helped with this healing as I've learned how not to be a victim to them, but rather a vessel for their full expression.

Emotions are the sensations we feel in our bodies, while feelings are the thoughts we have about our emotions. All emotions and feelings have a vibration to them, some low in vibration, or "negative," others high in vibration, or "positive." As everything emits energy, either positive or negative, emotions and feelings are no different, and in fact are far more powerful in how they shape our lives than we may be aware.

According to David R. Hawkins, who has written extensively about this range of emotions, peace is the most high-vibrational emotion in humans. In his life-changing book *Letting Go*, he describes a scale of emotions that correspond with levels of consciousness. Shame, the lowest of emotions, measures at twenty calibrations, while enlightenment, the highest emotion, measures at one thousand. The scale moves from shame to guilt, then apathy, grief, fear, desire, anger, pride, courage, neutrality, willingness, acceptance, reason, love, joy, and peace.[20]

Courage is the tipping point from lower, negative emotions to the higher, positive ones. Courage can be achieved from any lower emotion simply by being willing to look at, accept, and surrender whatever feels dense in the moment. When we acknowledge the sensations of our body, rather than suppressing, ignoring, or fighting against them, we rise in our vibration immediately. Life expands and radiates immeasurably when peace becomes a bigger goal than being right, having pride, being locked into old stories of humiliation or trauma, playing the victim archetype, feeding greed, depending on or blaming others, feeling anxious about the future, regretting the past, or thinking life is hopeless.

When we let go of the lower emotions and rise into the higher states of love, peace, joy, acceptance, and bliss, our path opens up, life becomes a wondrous offering of opportunities, and we find that our purpose, career, and service is a joyful expression of our naturally abundant being. It's only when we dwell in negative states that we feel lost, cannot find our way, miss out on opportunities, feel taken advantage of, and never fully release our past. When we consistently reach for courage, we feel more creative in the ways in which we can show up for ourselves and those we love and serve. Our purpose becomes clear each day because we're tuning in to our heart, the center of all emotions, the gateway to our Soul.

Living with a welcoming attitude toward emotions will expand the potential of your path and allow your light to guide you toward all that is meant for you.

20.   David R. Hawkins, *Letting Go: The Pathway of Surrender* (Carlsbad, CA: Hay House, 2012), 28–32.

Open-hearted healing is an important part of your purpose, because without it, you may never fully know your highest potential and deepest truth.

· RITUAL ·
Surrendering the Density

I've wasted far too many days and weeks suppressing unwanted, negative emotions, or fighting their existence. The more I would argue with or resent them, the stronger they would become—if not immediately, then at a later time.

The ritual I use is unbelievably simple and helpful and clears the way for my path to be seen. It's inspired by the processes of *Letting Go*.

Start this ritual whenever an uncomfortable emotion presents itself in your body. Here's how simple it is: all you need to do is feel it fully and let it go. Allow the emotion to come alive in your body without any thoughts attached to it, then let it go.

I use this ritual for emotions, soreness in my body, sickness, and any other discomfort that I sense physically. I believe our thoughts play a role in the creation of our body's emotions, aches, and illnesses, and in the act of surrender, much of the discomfort, and even the sickness and illness, is able to dissipate.

I also believe that miracles happen through loving surrender. When you surrender what is weighing you down, you'll find positive emotions like bliss and peace have a chance to bloom fully within, and the Universe is then able to bring to you all that is meant for you.

Keep letting go of whatever feels dark and heavy so that you may be so wondrously full of your own luminous light.

Anchoring into Your Place

Knowing your place in your community is both empowering and humbling. It's calling on the brave wisdom within you to be shared and it's also opening to a deeper listening to those around you. Knowing your place is more than knowing your gifts and talents, your name and qualifications; it's feeling into the land where you live, listening to the spirit of the place, and honoring what comes from the connection with your community and the place you call home.

• Journey •
Rising Sun, Setting Moon

Imagine a bright, clear morning after a full moon, and with joyful serenity, you wake with the sunrise.

Slipping out of your tent to stretch your body on the beach, leaving your beloved to sleep soundly, you relish a moment of gentle, all-over radiance. The rising golden sun shines into your sleepy face and soft heartspace, the setting moon glows at your back.

You feel held by these two magnificent forces.

In this moment, you know your place. You know the direction you are facing and all the directions around you. You connect with and give thanks for them all. You connect with reverence to the Mother holding your feet every day, you connect with the sky of gleaming stars and bright blues watching you from above. Last, you connect with the heart and Soul within you, your feeling of home and access to all wisdom and love.

Now that you feel steadier on the ground, you know how you wish to live the next phase of your purpose in this new community you call home.

The healing flames are pulling you closer in… closer to them, to your purpose, to your multidimensional gifts, and to the people who need them. You recall the visions you had months ago of serving with the golden flames of healing. These dreams and visions come back to you now, and you're able to tangibly feel them activating within you as you stand between the rising sun and sinking moon. The light beaming all around you initiates you into a new purpose that begins today.

You bask in the salt water for a while, then eat breakfast with your love.

With a renewed zest and focus on your mission and a stronger light glowing in your heartspace, you both head back to your community.

The Wisdom of the Land

When it comes to knowing my place, one practice has surprised me with its potency and connection. It's the practice of connecting with the wisdom of the land. Anytime I feel unbalanced or lost on my path, I connect mindfully with nature's spirited beings and feel immediately grounded, powerful, and one with the cosmos, wherever I am. I consciously sit with a tree, sink into a rock pool, walk with bare feet on stones, dirt, and grass, delight in new blooms and growth, and listen to the elements.

Living on sacred land in Bundjalung Country, Australia, has called me to reverently merge with nature each day, share my offerings, bless the elements, and listen to *the wisdom of the land* that seeps into my being. If I don't, I feel out of balance, unsettled, sleepless, and edgy. When I tangibly feel into my place on earth, I feel more at home, more connected to who I am in this body. This overflows into my career, providing a loving sense of importance and a strong feeling of service.

From this place of connection, I'm naturally inspired by my community to hold space through mentoring sessions, meditative journeys, sacred circles, and women's retreats. It's not only these purposefully created periods, but also the intentional moments of sharing smiles, love, laughter, hugs, and listening that draw me into a more genuine and palpable way of being with my community.

Every morning on waking, there is a message from the Ancient Ones of this land, and in the evening, there is a calling for me to share my gratitude with them and all Nature Spirits here. In between, I spend my days following the intuitive compass within my heart while honoring the elements at play on the land.

By listening to the elements, I find myself more in tune with the inner pull within my elemental being. By leaning into the wind, I feel stronger. By speaking to the rain, I am nourished. By receiving the rays of sun and fire, I feel the radiance of Spirit grow within me. By standing firm with the earth, I feel more stable in my body. By praying for harmony with all elements, I feel at ease within myself.

As humans, we have an inherent connection with the elements.

Each element has its own spirit who is always listening to our prayers. It's up to us to pray each day, mindfully connect, ask for what we need, and give thanks. Every place on earth has its own ancestors, a long line of people who lived intimately with the earth and all living creatures. These sacred places have a voice to guide us if we only create space to listen. It's up to us to remember how connected and how powerful we truly are—and to live in accordance with *the wisdom of the land*.

· RITUAL ·
Sacred Discovery of Place

Wherever you live, it's on or near sacred land. Find out the Indigenous name of the land, the name of the people who lived there originally, and anything else that feels important. Each day, try one or many of these rituals to feel deeper into your sense of place:

- In a gentle morning meditation, listen to the spirit around your home that comes from the land. Connect with the wind if you can hear it. Write down what you see, hear, or know from this spirit.

- Walk with bare feet in nature around your home or close by. Ask to be nourished by the land as you walk slowly and mindfully. Send love and gratitude to the layers of sacred soil that support you.

- Bless the natural waterways on or near your home. Bless the beach, creeks, rivers, rock pools, waterfalls, and springs. If there are no natural sources of water, place a large shell or fountain in/on your yard or balcony, and keep the water fresh when it's not raining. Each day, bless the water, ask to receive blessings from all sources of water, and bless each glass of water you pour for yourself.

- Light a candle at night and meditate for a few minutes on the flame, using it to ignite a brighter flame within your being.

- As the sun sets, take an offering to nature, wherever you're guided to go. Give thanks for your day and ask for protection and a more tangible and blessed connection to your purpose. Your offering could be a crystal that you're not aligned with anymore, a shell, some incense, a prayer, or a dried leaf from a native tree.

With each day you devote to your rituals, notice your mood, how well you sleep, your energy levels, and if your purpose becomes more authentic, genuine, and from the heart.

Embody and Activate Light Codes

The sun has so much to offer us; from its warmth and life-giving energy to its daily light and joy, it's a source of life and delight to humans all over earth. Our beloved sun is also a spiritual source of light, meaning it holds and sends codes to us from the cosmos. Our sun is a gateway; it's a portal to consciously reach the rest of the Universe. It's also a portal for the rest of the cosmos to send light, codes, wisdom, and activations to us. Not only is the sun itself wise and generous, it's an amplifier of infinite consciousness as well. We have so much to learn and gain from connecting with the sun.

· JOURNEY ·
Light Codes and Ancient Minerals

It's a warm fall day on the next stretch of your ethereal journey. You've been sharing your healing with your community around the fire each night, calling on the sacred flames to ignite alchemy and lightness within each person who sits with you.

You've taken a day off to recharge your light, and you're following inner nudges over rocks and hills, searching for a cool crevice to sit within. Eventually you give up and lie on a rock that faces west. As your breathing slows, you hear whispers from the rock beneath you. A language so slow you can barely fathom the words.

Soon you're able to receive the message of the wide, flat, ancient being holding you.

"Look ahead," the rock speaks. "What do you see?"

"Plenty of other rocks," you reply, confused and curious.

"Open your inner eye and look into them. What can you sense is there?"

Without thought, only knowing, you reply, "Crystals!"

Suddenly immune to the blazing heat, you clamber over the rocks until you find what your Soul is looking for: a chamber of clear quartz crystals. Pulling rock after rock out of the way, you gently enter the shade of this cool hollow, careful not to break anything here in this luminous space. Sitting among the smooth, crystalline walls, you feel quenched, refreshed, and nourished.

You've held plenty of crystals in your time as a seeker and healer, but you've never sat or rested *within* one.

Your body rests deeply; in dreams, you recall your role as a Shaman in a previous life on these hills. You see the various hot springs, water holes, crystal caves, and an underground temples you built with your community.

You remember the people who would come to you for healing, to be held in such deep and reverent love that their bodies would naturally come to wholeness. Some of these Souls you recognize from your current life, and you understand why life has reconnected you: for love, service, and wisdom.

In your dream state, you begin to speak in a dialect foreign to your present self. It flows fluidly from you, a healing repertoire of sound that creates much ease and grace in the hearts of those present. You speak this until you are awake once more, receiving the gifts of a golden sunset over the sacred hills.

Suddenly your eyes are pierced with an otherworldly light beaming straight at you. Dazed, you open your eyes to see the sun permeating the crystalline rock surrounding you. You catch your breath as you look around to witness the matrix of light illuminated by the sun. Every color is flowing, a kaleidoscope streaming in all directions.

You close your eyes a little to dim the overwhelming flare of the sun's rays. As you do, your third eye opens to witness the light codes activated within. Aspects of your being come to life through the alchemy of light and crystal vibration. Ripples of bliss move through your being; pulses of the highest frequency reach into your core and activate your aura. The light language of your dreams falls from your lips, much louder now, echoing in the chamber of light and providing comfort and wisdom beyond this world.

After the light fades, you lie still, stunned at the treasures discovered today, taking time to integrate all that has been given to you through earth and sun.

The Light of Sun, Source, and Self

We all have one thing in common: our light. Our likeness, our oneness, is made of the most unfathomable, illustrious light. Our individual expression of this light from Source is coded within our own unique Soul. We're all the same and yet so breathtakingly unique.

There are many Souls who have come to earth at this time to assist their communities through this great awakening. They know their purpose is to walk their spiritual path and share the wisdom, the light, they receive along their journey.

A part of your gifts and job description as a conscious being of light is to regularly receive upgrades, a natural occurrence that is happening more and more regularly as Mother Earth ascends and Her energy activates from within Her and us.

We're all third-dimensional beings, as is all of nature. We are deeply connected and dependent on the second dimension, the crust and dirt of the earth. We are also powerfully connected to the first dimension, the core of Gaia. This time of awakening on earth is an opportunity for us to lovingly ascend through the fourth dimension of thought and archetypes into the fifth dimension (5D) of love and oneness. This involves becoming conscious of fearful narratives—especially from the media—and reclaiming our thoughts by focusing them on what's real and true for us, namely nature, family, community, and love.

Barbara Hand Clow explains the dimensions and our awakening with the earth better than anyone I know. In her phenomenal book *Alchemy of Nine Dimensions,* she writes about each dimension in exquisite detail. Barbara also explains the phenomenon of the spiral band of light called the Photon Band. This spiral is awakening us and the earth as our planet moves into this band of energy for the next two thousand or so years.

"Photons are conscious in some way. Photons are particles of light that vibrate with frequency waves, which carry the full spectrum of electromagnetic radiation…an unusually large amount of high-frequency photons are coming to our solar system…It is possible there is an increase that has something to do with the mysterious Photon Band."[21]

As our solar system moves into a galactic field of intense light, consciousness must expand and grow, for consciousness *is* light. This means our planet will evolve into a higher vibration that will not allow voracious negativity to control people, animals,

21.   Barbara Hand Clow, *Alchemy of Nine Dimensions: The 2011/2012 Prophecies and Nine Dimensions of Consciousness* (Charlottesville, VA: Hampton Roads, 2004), 71.

elements, vegetation, or earth's resources any longer. What this means for us is that nothing can be hidden in the growing light, not greed or darkness, not trauma or fear, not even individual thought. All will be seen in the eyes of loving transparency.

As you notice flowers and ferns speaking more directly to your heart, you're actively moving into the 5D. When you take time to feel the guidance and healing pouring from every tree and bird, you're living more connected to the 5D. When you sense the heightened energies of crystals, the sun and stars, homegrown food, hugs with loved ones, and soulfully crafted music, you're sensing 5D on earth. Every time you use your hands to take care of the earth and to use nourishment from the earth to take care of others, you're sharing your light with the land and nature beings all around you. There's a tangible sharing of light in the 5D that you feel as you expand your own radiance.

This planet has moved through a dark night of the Soul and is ready to spin into the light once more, to ready itself for a Golden Age of multidimensional beings living in community, celebrating each other and the land, living simply, lovingly, and highly attuned to Spirit.

You are an important part of this transformation, and light activations within your DNA will assist you at every step, giving you the ability to absorb and share higher-dimensional light. These activations occur within each cell. Your mind, body, and spirit are all energy fields around the core light of your Soul. As you welcome in more light to this multilayered field of light through activations, you ascend to a higher way of being; you move through the 4D to reach the 5D (and beyond) more often.

Although it's tempting to look up when feeling into the higher dimensions, they aren't above your head; they're all within the layers of light radiating from your Soul. Experiencing the dimensions

externally, above and below you, is powerful, but this is a representation of the multidimensional being within you. With activations, you're able to access these within you more easily; you'll feel
and sense them. This can feel like intoxicating love, like pulsating
energy radiating through your body, like a clearer mind, or you
may sense it through telepathy or psychic awareness.

I've felt subtle activations during long hugs, intuitive yoga, and
quiet meditations. I've felt wonderfully intense activations through
the morning sun, energy and sound healings, and conscious connection with nature.

There is no sure way of making an activation happen, though
honoring daily rituals in nature, listening to healing sounds, and
regular energy healings help. There are many other practices you
can try if you're drawn to them, from breathwork practices and
sacred geometry to crystal grids and activating visualizations. If
you are on your spiritual path, letting go of old ways and stepping
into newness, you are naturally vibrating higher and activations
will occur, whether you realize it or not.

If you're curious about what is stored in the eternally expansive light of your being, you can access your Akashic records in
meditation or with a guide to discover more of what you need to
know, but rarely will you be able to fully fathom the wisdom, intelligence, love, and perfection of your illuminated essence (luminescence) through your human mind. Meditation practices can help
you transcend the mind and experience your light from a higher
state of awareness.

Your luminescence holds your purpose *and* the power of
Source energy to activate this purpose in this lifetime. You are so
intimately and intricately designed to fulfill your purpose.

You are the light of sun, Source, and self.

That's why I adore and believe in the power of serendipity. Life has a way of gathering wildflowers and delivering them to you when you need them. When you're learning and loving, sharing and contributing, and intentionally living life to the best and highest of your abilities, life will meet you with all you need. Life will summon the right gifts, tools, people, and situations to bring your purpose into its full realization.

There are no accidents or mistakes. Those who are meant for you will find you and dance the beautiful dance of loving reciprocity with you. The way of your heart will wend and weave until it finds you, takes your hand, and shows you the way. The gifts that are coded in the light of your being will nudge you and show up in your dreamtime until you honor them as your purpose and live them every day.

The more you listen to the loving, gentle, and wise voice within your heartspace and follow the opportunities that align with that voice, the more your inner pathways of light will vibrate at a higher frequency, which will attract like-hearted people, financial prosperity, greater well-being, awe-inspired awareness, and blissful moments.

· RITUAL ·
Light Code Activation

The best way I know to activate the light codes within, the very essence of your being that brings conscious awareness, divine intelligence, and pure healing into your form, is to sit with the morning sun.

This ritual can be done on the beach, in the forest, in your home, on your balcony, wherever you wish to access the rays of sunrise. Meditating on a vision of the sun's light can be a powerful process, too, but whenever you can, go outside and connect to the true sun; there is no substitute. Move through these steps intuitively:

1. Look at the sun as it ascends above the horizon (through your eyelids if you prefer).

2. Open your heart to the light; let your breathing be soft and long.

3. Repeat this mantra:

> I am light. I welcome divine light from the sun, the Great Central Sun, and Source energy into my being. I ask for gentle, powerful rays of light to move through me now to activate my radiant light being. All is perfect in this moment. My light is in harmony with Source and I receive all I need. And so it is.

4. You may feel tingling or bliss or a more subtle experience. Let go of expectations and trust that your light is activating. Notice what occurs throughout the day that follows. Allow this ritual to weave itself into each morning or whenever you naturally rise early.

FOLLOW YOUR GALACTIC CONSTELLATIONS

For many of us, the stars in the sky, the sparkling planets where we have incarnated many times before, feel like home. In the constellations and galaxies, we are connected to past lives and ancestral wisdom that can be beneficial to our purpose in this lifetime on earth. There are many ways in which you can connect to the stars and learn more about your gifts and purpose. If you wish, go deeply into the following journey with an open heart and mind, so you can connect with and receive the benefits of the many compassionate star beings who walk beside you.

· JOURNEY ·

Eternal Reaches of Starlight

Visualize yourself in a tent late at night, restless, unable to comply with the rhythm of sleep. You rise quietly out of your tent, warm woolens around your shoulders, to sit in nature and empty your mind.

Propping your soft, sleepless form against the support of a large boulder, you close your eyes halfway as you gaze into the guiding lights of the deep, endless sky. Each star gazes back at you, directly into your being, causing a stirring of your luminous past, a remembering of your origins.

Time dissolves; the earth beneath you seems to fall away. Your Soul expands with the emergence of your inner star and encapsulates your form. A bevy of beings leave their place of residence in the astrology of the night to come sit with you in a circle. Within this Star Council, you exchange galactic information, ancestral remembrance, and light language. Your whole being overflows with familiarity.

Your Soul recalibrates with ancient codes of light. The subtle knowingness of your being burns stronger, brighter, with a cause beyond words.

Bathing in the glow of your star family, you sit in this space of reverence and awe for an infinite pause.

Your eyes slowly close, the stars return to their place in the cosmos, and your body rests deeply to appreciate this heavenly glow.

Eventually the sun finds you asleep against the rock and warms you from the crown of your glorious being to the tips of your toes. You feel resurrected, and in no rush to move or forget the night's celestial gathering.

CONNECTING WITH THE
WISDOM OF STARS

If you've ever met someone who is lucidly connected to the land—any land, in any country—chances are they're going to have a *lot* to tell you about the stars. If you've ever had the utter privilege of sitting with an Indigenous Elder or Shaman, you'll know the timeless depths they've traversed through the earth and stars, you'll have heard stories of the ancestors of blood and starlight that mingle in their bones, and you'll remember the healing presence of simply *being* with one so connected.

The Ancient Ones created the original calendars from the movement of stars—and our movement relative to the stars—as well as with the cycles of the moon and sun.

The only past-life regression I've ever had that showed me a life not on this planet was a pure remembering of starlight. It came as a surprise to both myself and Eliza, my regressionist; I was simply and wondrously a light being. My speech was slow, a rare feat for this fast-talking human. During the regression, I was in such a high-dimensional state that attempting to put into words the encounter as my innocent and pure star self felt like a huge stretch for my mind. I wanted to experience it without words, but for the sake of the experience, I needed to elucidate my adventure verbally.

I could sense I was part of a group of light beings—Soul family—newly born from Source energy. It seemed like we fell from this impossibly luminous light as a cluster. I felt so delicate, perfect, sublime, innocent, and happy. I could tell that my light self was invisible, and that I would eventually incarnate in a "place," but initially I was timeless, formless energy.

As we beings gathered around each other, Source energy would send pulses of sacred geometrical intelligence into our fields for us to radiate out into the Universe wherever it needed to go. There was no thought process as such, more of a gentle impulse to receive, amplify, and share.

When Eliza asked me to move ahead to an important moment in my "life," although this was what I believed to be the beginning of all my lives, I saw my first incarnation as a star. I merged fully with a small star and felt what pure radiance feels like. And like a human discovering the absolute joy of learning to ride a horse, I blissfully sent my star flying through the night sky.

I imagine the unrepeatable set of codes we each carry through our incarnations are a prismatic combination of sacred geometry, light language, and immeasurable divinity. Discovering your star sign, star family, or star origins can be a revealing and insightful connection as you deepen into living your purpose. It can provide you with information about who you are on your deepest level, why you're here, what gifts you carry with you, as well as the challenges you may have incarnated to work and love your way through.

Not all the work done with stars is conscious; much of it is in our unconscious mind and spiritual domains. When you set an intention to live more aligned with the stars, you'll live more as the luminous galactic being you are and receive more of what the stars wish to share with you. You'll feel the pull to spend time with the visible stars in the night sky, lying at their feet, witnessing their sparkle, and allowing their magic to move through your light body. You'll be able to call on their glints of divine brilliance to light your path and show you the way toward higher states of peace and unity. You'll discover a deeper trust in the unseen activations received from each beloved star family member.

You'll relish the higher frequency of *connecting with the wisdom of stars*.

You may even feel called to connect consciously to Lyra, Sirius, Arcturus, and the Pleiadian star systems (among others). There's endless information available online about these and many more star races; just listen to your intuition. Your heart will tell you who is bringing through the highest information for your benefit. You may even connect to more than one star race, depending on where you've incarnated the most in the cosmos and who agreed to walk beside you from your star families.

During the day, we are able to receive codes from our glorious sun, a star from the Pleiadian system. Night and day, stars surround us, offering powerful portals to light, to the source of all life. It's important that we regularly pause to connect with, recharge from, and integrate the seen and unseen sources of light into our light codes.

To consistently rejuvenate your spirit, the most vibrant reality of your being, is essential on your journey.

Between the activations, initiations, downloads, and service, you'll find the need for calm, timeless pauses. These will bring you a higher expression of energy and a more definitive version of you that reaches beyond logic, time, and space.

Your everyday purpose is to shine your starlight brighter. You do this by speaking your truth, sharing your gifts, roaming in the wilderness within and all around you, and persistently seeking joy. You do this by following what lights you up because it literally does. You do this by embracing the star being you've always been, always will be, and always have access to.

· PRACTICE ·

Star Origins Soul Prompts

If you're curious about your star ancestry, you can use the following journal prompts to discover where you originated from, who is here to help you, how your lives in various star systems and galaxies have prepared you for this one, and any gifts you have from these cosmic places. Take out your journal, flip to a fresh page, and enjoy where these take you.

- Ask your star family to reveal itself to you in signs, symbols, and messages. Keep your mind open and your eyes aware of any messages from the Pleiadians, Sirians, Andromedans, Arcturians, and Lyrans (five of the most common, benevolent ancestors to humans) as you go throughout your day. You may have books come into your awareness, or conversations, symbols, images or messages online, or dreams. Write them down as you see them and note how they make you feel.

- As your star families come into your life, you can set a conscious intention to connect with the benevolent beings who represent each lineage. Freewriting is an effective way of bringing through their messages, especially when done early in the morning as the dawn is breaking and your mind is soft and uncluttered. Write at the top of the page the name of the star system, such as Sirius, or even a planet, such as Venus, that has been getting your attention. Let your hand flow with notes that may ring true immediately or not make sense at the time but will inevitably be important on your path. Ask for advice on your Soul's purpose and what steps to take as you walk your path under their stellar guidance.

- Connect with one star in the sky before you go to bed each night. Stand or lie underneath it and simply feel the light pouring down to your being. Send all your wishes to the heart of that star and know that they have already been granted. Ask them to visit you in your dreams and that you remember them. Write down any ideas, visions, or messages that come to you.

Keep taking notes in your journal of what you see and learn, how deep the connection feels, and any dreams you may have. Know and believe you are protected from any being who does not have your highest interest at heart by always asking for benevolent beings. And always give thanks.

Chapter 10

EMBRACE DIVINE IMPERFECTIONS

*"When you are in conflict or doubt, or afraid ... move beyond the
pain and fear, there is an awareness there ... And in spite of its
ethereal and indefinable nature, we all know that it's love."*[22]
—RUSSELL BRAND

Many people fear being rejected, failing in their career, or appearing as anything other than perfect in their own eyes or in the reflection of another. If only we could *embrace* aloneness, quirkiness, rejection, failure, and imperfection. Wouldn't that be the most empowering way to live? Wouldn't that be the freedom that gives us permission to really *go for it?*

There may be times in your career—no matter how abundant, creative, affluent, innovative, aligned, rewarding, or meaningful—when you will be alone, you will be rejected, you will fail, and you will seem imperfect.

Relax in this knowing: it's in these moments when you're being transformed or redirected onto another route. *Relish* these moments when you can, knowing you've been given a clear sign

---

22.   Russell Brand, *Revolution* (London: Arrow, 2015), 353.

to go within and reset your compass, cleanse your energy, sharpen your focus, or reassess your connections.

In the space of loving acceptance, you will rise above the ego's resistance and outrage into a softer and more powerful way of being.

This chapter is devoted to the mess inherent in living your Soul's purpose and how to face it with courage and grace.

KNOW THE EXQUISITE BEAUTY OF FAILURE

If we could only cut out the shame and guilt normally associated with failure and unexpected outcomes, we would see what a gift they are on our path. Failure is fire. Your purpose is like lead that becomes redefined, alchemized, and illuminated in the fire, turning to gold and becoming much more valuable and medicinal to all you meet.

· JOURNEY ·
Sacred Mandala of Forgiveness

You find yourself at the beginning of summer with a burning mission. In your excitable quest to create a temple for the upcoming summer solstice, you overlook the wisdom of those around you—and your own heart—to create a completely open-air space, and instead decide to build a covered wooden shelter that lines up with the rising solstice sun.

You take available wood and make a floor, pillars, and a roof. This takes a week with the help of a few others—who caution you to choose a different type of wood (more wisdom disregarded in haste)—to help make it as stable as possible.

When the structure is finished you take a stroll to find dried grass for the thatched roof. On your return, you see some of the temple's wood has already cracked and the overall anatomy seems unstable. You're frustrated at yourself for not designing it properly or listening to other builders in your community.

Unsure of how to progress safely without having to remake the entire temple, you take a walk to the nearest water hole and immerse yourself in the cooling, satiating, cleansing waters. As you sit next to the water to dry off in the filtered sun, a squabble of gulls have a good laugh in spite of your frustration. Their song is contagious, and soon you are laughing along with them.

Still ambivalent about what to do with your careless construction, but unattached to it and feeling much lighter, you head back to your camp to humbly consult your community.

When you reach the site of your temple, everything is gone except for a fractured floor. Curious, you look around to see your brothers and sisters setting up a ceremony site in a clearing. When you ask them about the temple, they tell you that the pillars fractured and the roof collapsed; without you around to refer to, they decided to use your soft, smooth wood for seating around a summer flower mandala. The roof's grass is in a bowl with lavender, ready for an energy clearing tomorrow morning, the day of the solstice.

You smile in gratitude as someone hands you a cup of tea with calendula flowers. Your perceived failure has been transformed into a beautiful, sacred space. As you finish your tea and gather a bunch of fresh flowers in your arms, you help place them in a softly geometric shape with your beloved and all who are contributing. The outcome is a far more stunning gift to honor the energy of summer than you could have envisaged on your own, and your gratitude and anticipation bloom in preparation for tomorrow's ceremony.

LEARNING DURING MISADVENTURE

With the beauty and clarity of hindsight, I can see how many of my misadventures were actually perfect. They always, somehow, delivered me to the place I was meant to be.

I was incredibly disappointed in my high school result. My overall marks meant I couldn't apply for what I thought I wanted to study at university; however, they were enough to apply for a bachelor of arts, which was the most perfect three-year journey of psychology, sociology, philosophy, religion, architecture, and so much more. My entire life changed during that degree, and it's been invaluable to me ever since.

When I completed my degree, I wasn't able to enroll in an honors program in psychology due to my grades. That felt like failure for a little while until I remembered I gave my all at university for three years, I have a degree I'm proud of, and life is taking me somewhere else more suited to my gifts.

Throughout my working career, there have been failures, challenges, embarrassments, and frustrations. None of them have been fun, but I can see how mysteriously perfect each outcome was, and how deeply I *learned through misadventure*.

I strongly believe there is no such thing as failure (besides exam results)—only the Universe showing you what's not for you or where you need a little more loving attention. I also believe that rejection is never personal and only ever a sign that whoever is rejecting you is out of alignment with your energy. Failure certainly doesn't mean you're bad at anything, and rejection doesn't mean you're worse than anyone else. It's simple energetics: either a person or an offering is able to flow into your field or it's not. If you still want whatever you failed at or whomever rejected you, have a loving look at whether it's your ego chasing something that's not right for you (denser energy), or if you need to heal, grow, and transform in order to match what you're desiring (lighter energy).

No matter what happens or how powerless you feel during times of exclusion, abandonment, defeat, breakdowns, and frustration, you *always* have the opportunity to accept whatever happens, see it as a valuable lesson, and pivot toward optimum and optimistic possibilities.

Failures come and go on the messy, mysterious path of life. Allow them to teach you as you navigate with grace and humor, and let go of the belief that hardship and struggle are a necessary part of life, or on the flipside, that your job needs to be perfect to be successful. Your mindset goes a long way to smoothing out the trails of destiny. Your Soul lessons, karma, initiations, and relationships will give you plenty to learn from, but if you carry around a negative mindset or expect perfection, this will make the journey unnecessarily difficult and disappointing.

In your career, you may lose jobs, miss out on promotions, clash with coworkers, struggle financially, question your skills, or be taken advantage of. You may start your own company and need to close it soon after it opens. You may go into business with someone and lose intellectual property or creative rights. You may become outrageously successful very quickly and struggle with the sudden changes. There are endless ways to feel at a loss, but with fewer attachments to rigid outcomes and more flexibility around success coming to you in a plethora of ways, your energy will fluidly adapt and expand with each hurdle.

Gently sweep away failure as an identity or an option. You are not a failure, nor have you ever been. Let that fragmented thought go. And looking ahead, know deep in your bones and in the spark of your Soul that *you cannot fail*. You're navigating this life the best you can—you're *learning through misadventure,* as is everyone else. Have compassion, especially for yourself, when hard times arrive.

When one door closes, leave the building altogether and head for nature; walk the wildhearted way where there are no doors to open, no glass ceilings to burst through, no ladders to climb, and no hallways to wander, isolated and alone. Learn about your nature from Mother Earth. In Her there is no failure or rejection, only love and appreciation for all who show up with an open heart.

· PRACTICE ·
Loving Hindsight Soul Prompts

Take out your notebook and write down six moments in your life that felt like failure or rejection. Choose one event that still feels painful or try the following process gently and gratefully with all six:

1. Start with writing down what happened and how it "failed" or how you were "rejected." Without blame, write where you were, who was involved, what you wanted, and why you didn't get the outcome you desired.

2. Now look at the situation not from within it, but rather from above it, and write what you see from an impersonal, higher presence. Notice what attachments you had to people, ideas, or outcomes that caused you to label the situation or event as a failure.

3. See the moment from someone else's perspective. Put yourself in the shoes of another person who was involved but unaffected. Write about the event from their eyes.

4. Expand your memory of the event to include a blessing that happened afterward that couldn't have hap-

pened if everything had worked out as you'd hoped. Often with rejection and failure, there's a loss, and in the loss, we feel empty. Through this emptiness, the Universe delivers a higher magic that we didn't have the capacity to receive previously.

5. Finish with a healing process. Send love and forgiveness to all involved, including and especially to yourself.

THE MUSE OF THE IMPERFECT WILDFLOWER

I once dreamed I was an old woman. In the dream, I had been through a personal initiation into cronehood. After this process, I walked through my local town with such strength, beauty, and power that I haven't yet felt in this body, in this life. I looked to other elderly women with such heartfelt reverence and a knowing that we were the quiet, unassuming, and all-powerful goddesses and mystery keepers of our community. Since the dream, I've looked to older women with such adoration, and I've grown even more at ease with what I see changing in the mirror … and in all of nature.

• JOURNEY •
Reflections in Creation

Imagine yourself after all this time spent in nature with long, disheveled hair. You mention the state of your locks to a friend and they offer to cut them for you. It's been so long since you had a fresh trim, and the opportunity sounds like heaven. With gratitude and an herb garden in exchange, you meet.

When your hair is neat and your scalp massaged, when your locks are shiny and clean, you fold the fallen hair in a large leaf with flowers and herbs. You tuck this into your pocket to give to nature as an offering later. Then your Soul sister passes you a mirror.

You haven't seen your face reflected in anything other than nature's still waters for so long, and the image is radiant to you. The lines on your face are more present, skin tanned, eyes shining bright; you look naturally vigorous.

Grateful for the fresh energy, you leave their hut only to see your reflection everywhere you go. The wildflowers beckon you into their garden, each one so remarkable. Gazing into their softness, you see the imperfect and rugged blossoming of your untamed beauty within their petals.

Later, while walking among the trees, you capture your essence in the strength of these companions. You feel how deeply your roots have grown, how high your energy has evolved.

At night, you grasp another likeness in the stars above. They shimmer on their own in the dark, independent of each other, yet all the more breathtaking when making magic and composing symbols together. You resonate with their individual perfection, cosmic interdependence, and incomparable fire.

There you are in the reflection of creation.

Most glorious of all, you see your perfection reflected back to you from the light within the eyes of your Soul family. Each of them connected to you, to the land, to their spirit, in their own fundamentally unique and perfect way.

ABUNDANCE OVER PERFECTION

If we simply and completely let go of the word *perfect*, then there cannot be *imperfection*.

When we let go of the false ideal of "perfection," then we remember the beautiful and profound truth: we're all precisely who and where we're meant to be on our own evolutionary journey.

Careers are often messy. Let them be. Revel unapologetically in the wonder of discovering and rediscovering purpose, service, and work a thousand times over.

The wilder your life becomes—whether you move into nature, rebel against expectations, or allow the light to grow unapologetically strong within you—the more you'll stop comparing yourself to others, judging something as good or bad, or expecting things to look a certain way.

Nature isn't good or bad, one flower can't be better than another, the sun doesn't compare itself to the moon, trees don't get revenge if their growth is cut off by a vine, and abundance flows as a natural law. Wildflowers are the ultimate muse. Perfection doesn't exist within the petals, stamens, and stems, and yet, they delight, surprise, heal, and revive us all.

Nature honors *abundance over perfection*.

In the early days of spring a few years ago, after spending more time at home than usual that year, I looked around my garden and, to my surprise, couldn't find *one* spring flower. I felt deflated. I knew that the frangipani and poincianas were to come in summer, but to have a spring without flowers in my own little garden felt lackluster and dreary.

The next time I met with my neighbor, an amazing gardener, I asked her if she could help me. I felt inarticulate in the language of flowers and needed her intuitive expertise. Her garden was falling over itself with beauty every day of the year, so I knew she'd be the perfect collaborator for my project.

By early spring the following year, I had more than thirty varieties of flowers blooming in my garden, and my heart and hands had discovered an easy communion with seeds, soil, and sunshine. The flowers were just starting to look colorful and plentiful by late that summer when we moved to the rainforest. I'm still trying not to be attached to whether they're cared for or not. All I know is, I gave them life and, in return, they rewilded a part of me.

Wildflowers will grow where they will grow. Cultivated flowers can be sown and loved anywhere that suits their needs. In between, there's the wildflower that's grown on purpose, to be wildish in a specific place for a particular person, family, or need; and then there's the cultivated flower that sends its seeds flying into the wind, sending their descendants to take root in fortuitous places. Neither better nor worse, all blooming as best as they can.

Taking your career and steering it exactly where you want it to go—with love and determination—is like buying the seeds of your favorite flower and giving them to a pot, planter, garden, or field. If it's meant to be, and with enough sunshine and water, they'll bloom for you. And with any luck, your chosen flowers, like your purposeful pursuits, will teach you a few things—namely, that life doesn't always turn out as you expect it to, you need to sow seeds if you want to dream big, and abundance everywhere is reflecting your essence back to you.

Flowers *are* abundant. And so are you. As Tosha Silver writes in *Outrageous Openness,* when it comes to embodying abundance, no matter your astrological imprint or the mood of the cosmos, "Without a feeling of expansion and contentment, even the blessings from the best of planetary transits won't matter, since abundance is something to be, not seek or await. If you embody generosity and flow, if you move from Divine Source, what needs to come will always come regardless of the stars or the insane economy."[23]

23. Tosha Silver, *Outrageous Openness: Letting the Divine Take the Lead* (New York: Simon & Schuster, 2014), 81.

Whether you listen to the flowers, your heart, the Goddess, or Source; whether you call on nature, love, stars, or Spirit, it's all supporting you to open and bloom.

· RITUAL ·

A Spiritual Prayer for All Wild Beings

I pray that you grow tall where you are
In the body that you've been blessed with
Knowing your light and beauty are infinite.
I pray that you open every petal wide
To reveal your truth to all who need it
As a mirror for the highest potential in all.
I pray that you hear the stars calling you
That you lie in the fullness of the sun
And you dance in the luminosity of the moon.
I pray that your purpose is shared
For the sake of your flowering heart
And the buds all around you.
I pray that when one cycle closes
You trust in the seeds that fly away
To birth new life again.
Blessed be.

Chapter 11
YOU ARE THE PURPOSE

"You're starting to understand no one else can see what you see.
Your life and your dream is yours, tucked up inside of you."[24]
—LAUREN ALETTA

In this final chapter, I want to remind you of what your heart already, always knows. You are magnificent; *completely* magnificent. *Everything* you need is within you. *You* are the purpose. And love is *all* there is.

If you're pushing and striving to get somewhere else, to be someone else, then you're missing out on the incredible wonder of who and where you are right now. In every moment, you are the Divine embodied, Source incarnate, and Love defined.

Humanity is blessed to have you here, walking among us all. Mother Earth is blessed to have you as part of Her vital expression. And your Soul family is blessed to be a companion to your light.

Keep living as incredible you, all of you, and nothing but you.

---

24.   Lauren Aletta, *Into the Woods* (Queensland, Australia: Inner Hue, 2017), 112.

LIFE AS A GRAND MASTER OR
HIGH PRIESTESS

We are living in a time on earth where the veil that has for so long kept us protected is thinning rapidly. The veil is a spiritual cloak that somewhat separates us in the physical realm from the higher, etheric realms. In the past, only a gifted few were able to pierce the veil to access the higher realms; these days, it's thin enough for anyone to do so. As our consciousness expands and our bodies become lighter (radiating a brighter Soul light), we are able to see through the veil and connect with higher wisdom. This may be wisdom from past lives, our ancestral lineage, star families, sacred geometry, light language, or other information held in the Akashic library. It's a powerful time to be alive.

· JOURNEY ·
Intuitive Rituals of Awakening

Along this next meditative adventure, you're experiencing dreams where you're meeting with past versions of you in ancient lives. During the day after each dream exploration, you hear echoes of chanting, singing, and stories from the dream that merge with your everyday reality. These rich sensory connections stay with you along your path and appear as though alive on the earth plane. You sense your Soul is prompting you to ignite a new ritual with nature.

You see your ancestors in nature. They speak to you, telling you their energy never completely leaves the earth; their bodies are an eternal part of it. When a body is fully decomposed, it fertilizes the soil, which creates new life. The legacy of a life can never be unwound from nature's aliveness. When you create and devote to rituals in nature, you're connecting to rituals with your past incarnations, your ancestral lineages, and the living spirits of Gaia.

One inspired morning, as the honeyed sun rises, you set an intention to gather all you need to create a ritual underneath the full moon that evening. You heed the call of your Soul to intuitively bring together what you need without having to know the details or purpose of the ritual. Your dreams have brought into your awareness the scope of your incarnations on earth and how connected you are to so many healing lineages.

After a cup of lemon myrtle tea, you discover a branch of dried eucalyptus leaves and put it aside. On your morning walk, you find rusty red clay and bloodred sap. While eating lunch, a flock of exuberant falcons come to squawk in a tree overhead and leave you with an immaculate, long, white-and-brown-spotted feather. And you notice a seedpod as you wake from your afternoon nap.

To refresh yourself, you take a naked swim in a river nearby. As you enter the cool water, you pause to bless your body, your life, and the waters that flow, cleanse, and nourish your being. Floating on a gentle current, you surrender all concerns. The sun sweeps through the trees, caressing your body, energizing inner wisdom for the ritual ahead.

As you walk from the river and consciously dress in soft white clothes, you feel as though the ritual has already begun. Body, senses, and spirit are refreshed. With renewed vitality, you intuitively create a circle of rocks and place kindling in the middle, lighting it with ease after all this time learning the ways of nature. The warmth from the fire dries your skin, and you pause in awe as a swarm of bees circles the fire before departing.

You pick up the gum leaves and set them alight, then blow out the flames and use the smoke to cleanse your energy. You take the spotted feather and brush it through the air as a fan to send the smoke in all directions. You call in your Ancestors, honoring them for the gifts they left for you in your blood and the earth, asking for their protection, guidance, love, and presence. You call on the Nature Spirits to come closer, to surround your sacred ritual with blessings. You call on the Spirit of the Elements, sharing your gratitude with them for their wisdom and mystery.

You pause to fully open your heart, allowing the inner flames to rise with the power and illumination of Spirit and all your past and future lives. You release all the binds and curses of all lifetimes, timelines, dimensions, and space. You bless the many aspects of your Soul and ask that all fragmented parts return to their place. And you send the overflowing gifts of this sacred ceremony to your beloved community.

Your beloved joins you, wearing the river's dappled beads, the softest white clothes, and a knowing smile. You cleanse and bless them in every way that you have done for yourself. The power intensifies, and you both radiate with shared luminosity.

Rubbing the clay and sap together, you place this balm on your love's third eye; they do the same on yours. Kneeling on the ground, you both touch your foreheads to the dusty earth in reverence for Goddess Gaia and all that She has provided for you on your journey.

Sitting back on your heels, you begin to sing a song in a language your mind doesn't understand but your Soul knows fluently. Your love joins in, harmonizing, humming, holding this sacred tune with you. As the sun colors the sky with its soft setting tones, this language of light streams from your lips and healing flows all around and within you. Closing your eyes, you begin to receive the wisdom of the stars.

You begin to cry healing, salty tears of awakening and remembering, feather and bone, moon and fire, Ancestors and Spirit.

As you fully relax into the softness of your being, your root chakra comes to life, energy moving up your spine and taking your breath away. You exhale with pleasure and notice many butter-flies coming to share in your bliss. You laugh in ecstasy with your beloved, and the fire bursts to life before your eyes. They take your hands and turn you around to show you the ripe, milky moon rising above the trees. Your heart erupts, love pouring out into the cosmos.

You dance in this joy with the leaves and the breeze and your beloved always close. Singing and swaying with your seedpods rat-tling into the night, the stars all celebrate your ritual of awakening.

Claim Your Power

It might have something to do with my astrology, my defiantly independent genes, or the rebellious nature of my Soul, but I have never been able to simply do as I'm told.

I carve my own path, beat my own drum, chant my own song, and dance to my own rhythm. If I want flowers, I'll plant them. If I want new friends, I'll go find them. If I need a new teacher, I'll call in someone deeply inspiring. If I want to learn something, I'll do a course or buy a book.

I cannot go a week without the insistent desire to discover, con-nect, and create.

Claiming my power is exciting and free, but it isn't always easy. I've lost friends, been cut off from family members, been turned down for dream jobs, and some days it feels like life is pushing up against my edges. But I cannot, will not, resist the pull of the wild within me.

On a short holiday for myself in a small cabin in Nimbin, Aus-tralia, just over an hour from where I live, I experienced a remem-bering of my own ancient priestess codes through ritual. I have always needed time alone to hear what my heart is saying, time to connect with Mother Nature and Spirit. While I was also there to relax, read books, and eat chocolate without interruption, my Soul had bigger plans.

I chose this particular place to visit in early 2021 because there was a waterfall on the property. Within a few minutes of arriving, hearing about the potential for meeting snakes, spiders, leeches, and ticks (all the creatures I now live with in the hinterland), I didn't feel a strong pull to walk to the falls straight away. I slept on it.

On the second day, my Soul spoke loudly. Without argument, I put my swimmers, dress, and boots on, grabbed my towel and phone, and walked up the hill.

The entire ten-minute walk was a prayer. Gratitude for the sacred pause. Permission from the Nature Spirits. Blessings for Gaia. Protection from the wild things. Calling in Ancestors. Surrendering all stress. Welcoming healing activations. Asking for forgiveness. Chatting with dragonflies.

My whole being rippled with bliss when I reached the falls. My timing was impeccable; not only had there been a lot of rainfall before my visit, but that afternoon the sun was ablaze.

When I stood close to the luscious waterfall, all thirty-five feet of flowing, feminine waters, I gasped. My being lit up. My smile was exaggerated and full. My feet danced on the spot.

I stood at the edge of her pool, all muddy and opaque, and thought this must be some kind of initiation into an unknown Mystery School. Without being able to see through the water, not even a little, I needed to let go of my fears and trust fully in Her, the Goddess.

I took my boots and dress off, stepped into the water, and surprised myself with a blessing that fell loud and clear from my lips:

I baptize myself in the name of the Goddess, in the name of all Goddesses, in the name of goddesses everywhere. I anoint myself; I am the sacred anointment and the anointed one. I am the Holy Grail. I purify myself and bless all beings everywhere on this glorious planet. And so it is.

I surrendered my body into the water, plunging three times into the murky depths. I felt renewed, alive, holy, courageous, and ecstatic. *I claimed my power.*

That baptism in nature revitalized every part of me. My commitment to nature deepened, my connection to the heart of Gaia strengthened, and my Soul's purpose grew.

And thankfully the only glimpse I had of a snake was a python's skin left for me on my last morning in the tree by my deck. I have it on my altar to remind me of the ways in which I can transform myself through a devoted connection to rituals and blessings in Gaia.

Walking my spiritual path requires me to take my power back from the religious ideology of my childhood, from my peers and teachers, from expectations, and from anyone who told me who I was meant to be and how I was meant to act.

My Soul's purpose cannot be fully experienced or expressed if I'm not living my empowered truth. If I am still hooked into the expectations of a guru or master, the needs or wants of a parent, the limitations of siblings or friends, the boxes of religion or conditional spirituality, or even my ego's constraints, then I cannot be the full and unrestrained expression of me.

That's my spirituality, to peel back the layers until I can feel the pure light of my Soul, see the raw beauty in my body, know the limitless wisdom of my mind, and live accordingly. When I do that, *everything* is on purpose.

Within every humble seeker is a Grand Master, High Priestess, or some other ancient leader, sage, mystic, oracle, guru, teacher, wayshower, poet, or healer. Let your body show you in nature all the rituals, song, listening, and ways that it remembers, imbued with soul-deep memories. The ancient mystery in you is ready to step out and lead as soon as you're ready to trust fully in its mastery.

Your mastery may be focused on one specific set of skills or many. Mastery doesn't mean you're the best at one particular skill; it means you've personally mastered it within yourself. It also doesn't mean you need to make money from it or share it with others, but if that's what you desire, go for it. Your mastery will look different to everyone else's; there's no sense comparing them.

Create space and time to receive messages from your Soul through the open channel of your heart every day so that you are able to follow the sacred knowing along your way with ease and faith.

I love to meditate and ask my Soul questions, then patiently wait for the answers in meditation or throughout the day. Sometimes the answers come in a song or a book, a conversation or a podcast, spontaneous insight or nature's messengers, oracle cards or during moments of inspired journaling. I trust I will discover all I need to know in divine timing.

Since the waterfall baptism, I regularly bless myself in rivers, creeks, rock pools, and the ocean. It's a ritual that brings more consciousness to my connectivity with water. I also love to mindfully kiss the earth with my feet, pray with the flowers that bloom in my garden, sing with the grand old trees, and dance with the fire in our rustic pit.

The High Priestess within is proud of me.

· PRACTICE ·
Ancient Self Soul Prompts

How would you describe your Soul's ancient self?

This is a practice for you to have a whole lot of fun with and hopefully remember—through the sacred medicine of joy and dreaming—who you are on the most magical and mystical level.

1. Take out your journal and let your imagination play with a description of your Soul's ancient self. Consider concepts of priest, priestess, goddess, master, fairy, warrior, wayshower, lightworker, and starseed. Which one feels the most aligned? How would you describe yourself in full? Try inspiring combinations, such as: Ancient Warrior of Fire, Holy Priestess of Light, Master of Alchemical Healing, Rainbow Fairy of Elemental Magic, Mermaid Lightworker of Oceania, or Galactic Starseed of Intercellular Awakening.

2. Now write a description of your purpose as this being. Make it bold or dreamy, entertaining or thoughtful, real or imaginary. Look at your life from your ancient self and allow messages to flow through your pen onto paper as a guide to your purpose.

3. If you're starting to sense something exciting landing in the realm of your journal, take a deeper dive into what you're noticing. Consider asking your Soul how you can adjust your daily habits and rituals to live more devotedly as your true self, or what is blocking your human self from living authentically.

This next practice involves oracle or tarot cards. If you have some, take out a deck that speaks to your purpose and the ancient description you just created.

1. Shuffle, cleanse, and intuitively choose four cards.
2. Your first card shows you the *highest purpose* and service of your Soul.
3. Your second card describes *where you are at* on your journey.
4. Your third card is all about the *blocks in the way* of you fully stepping into this purpose.
5. Your fourth card details what your *next step* may look or feel like.

You may want to consider the answers, journal with them, and place the cards on your altar for a week to let the symbolism and visuals guide your subconscious. Don't force or rush the momentum from this guidance; open to it and allow life to flow gently and generously in a higher direction.

The Whole Universe Is within You

There's a big difference between the earth we live on and the world we create in our minds. When I consider that the "world" is simply a hologram, an illusory representation or view of my beliefs, I begin to deepen my understanding and relationship with Mother Earth. It's our *earth* that's real; what presents to us as the "world" doesn't have any real substance. When it comes to the world, we see what we want to see, and this can fluctuate on a whim. It's our mysteriously, beautifully, surprisingly multidimensional planet that I relate to. When the world slips away, She's always there.

· JOURNEY ·
Kaleidoscopic Visions

Picture yourself after your personal, sacred ritual. Magic has been awakened within you, and now, as you look around, everything you see is more prismatic than usual.

In your beloved's eyes, you see the stars of their Soul's origins. With one hand on their belly, you feel the pulse of the earth. And when they smile, they shine like the sun.

You see butterfly wings on their back during times of deep transformation and the strength of old trees running through their spine. You feel the elements, the directions, the endless flora as a part of them.

And you know all of this to be true for you, too.

Everyone who sits with you for healing shows their true nature to you in their energy field before a word is spoken. You see lilies bloom from the palms of their hands, mushroom guides standing close by, hummingbirds whispering into their hearts, bears curled up on their lap, and tigers guarding them fiercely.

Mostly, they don't know any of this. So they come to you … for remembering, for healing, for space to cry and laugh and grieve, for a sacred pause to rest and open to their light. They come again and again … until they remember. Until they feel, see, and know the wild around them *as them*. Until the rising sun each morning reminds them of the awakening of the light of their Soul. Until they feel the stars as their own cells. Until they reverently breathe each breath as though it's the very lifeforce of the Universe.

KEEP FOLLOWING YOUR PRISMATIC LIGHT

You are the most amazing representation of the entire Universe. And yet, you are much more than a portrait, a copy, or an impression of the whole. You *are* the Universe.

It's imprinted on us from society that we're meant to search externally for the answers we need. We're meant to ask the government/politician, church/priest, ashram/guru, school/teacher, and company/boss for permission, compensation, or solutions on the prepaved road of society. It seems easy and comfortable at first, until you realize you're going in the same direction as everyone else and your heart's precious voice is lost in a sea of lifeless conformity.

The more energy you devote to your journey according to your inner cosmos, toward and on purpose, the freer you will feel. The role of Nature is to lure us into Her wildest parts so that we may undo all the conditioning and structures that limit our full expression and untether ourselves from everything that's holding us back. If you expect anything from the systems of the "world," you will trip over your own expectations. If you anchor solely into the galactic emanations of your Soul and the gifts of Mother Earth, you will live your most inspiring and abundant life.

You are the temple, the awakening, and the Universe. It's all in you. It always has been and always will be, in this and all lifetimes.

You don't need to be fluent in astrology to know your way around the Universe. You don't even need to call yourself "spiritual." Just *keep following your prismatic light* all the way home.

· PRACTICE ·

Live as the Universe Soul Prompts

Take out your notepad and feel into the powerful truth that you are the Universe.

- What is the wildest aspect of you and how is it reflected in nature? What do you love about this part?

- Where is your favorite place to go outdoors? How does it relate to your inner nature? How does it satisfy an inner yearning?

- What pieces of nature do you respectfully collect? Do you have crystals, rocks, feathers, shells, or seedpods in your home? How do they make you feel? What part of your personality do they represent? How do you connect into the energy of them? Are there any that need to be returned with gratitude to Mother Nature?

- How do you feel when witnessing the rising sun or full moon? What does a thunderstorm bring out in you? When was the last time you felt in awe of nature? When did you last pause in awe of your own incredible nature?

YOU ARE THE WILDHEARTED PURPOSE

You are the purpose. Everything you *do* when you are on purpose is magical, but it's who you *are* in your moments of pure authenticity and presence that truly lights up the cosmos.

· JOURNEY ·

The Way of the Healing Flames

Along this blissful stretch of your journey, you've reached a new-found state of everyday ecstasy. You meet with your beloved and other people within your community and feel the deepest love with a gentle touch, a smile, compassionate eye contact, a few words of loving kindness.

Everything feels gentle, serene, and yet the energy in your hands—and all the hands you're grateful to hold each day—is powerful. When you are *being* in your own presence and allowing that to be your greatest purpose, you are able to witness miracles unfold in your life.

Every day you show up on a grass mat in the shade, making endless cups of herbal tea. The tea is the bridge between you and those who are seeking your healing presence, your gentle, wise words, and your transformative hugs. These people sit with you all day—some for a few minutes, others for a few hours.

You find that the more you are present and listening, the more you're able to hold space for others to create a profound shift on their own. In some sessions you barely utter a word, in others you are filled with insight and inspiration from the highest reaches of your Soul.

After months of this relaxed and attentive level of service, you're able to teach those who have healed their traumas, egos, and pain, those who have transcended above the ordinary and into the mystical realms. You're able to show them the path of healing flames. You open a portal to share your own perspective on healing, and you also allow space for them to share this healing way through the honoring of their own gifts in their divine timing.

On occasion, a master of healing finds your community and sits with you all for a while. You learn from them as much as you can while they are around, but the most life-changing moments with them are in pure silence, where energies dance and flames flicker, where their loving presence washes away your edges and identity, and you feel into the limitlessness of being heaven on earth.

A GRAND AND WILD PURPOSE

Most of the time I have a sweet flow in my daily life. I live intuitively, not perfectly, so I have days when I rest and swim and days when I don't leave my computer for long. Most days are an unscheduled assortment of work, play, devotion, and pleasure.

There are weeks when I push against this flow. Sometimes these weeks feel deeply fulfilling among the busy-ness, knowing that life will naturally find its own harmony again. Other weeks feel like a struggle, sleep becomes fragmented, my body craves nature, and I rush my way toward some kind of real or perceived deadline.

When I'm feeling lost or unsure, disconnected or out of sync, I go to nature and feel into my place and purpose. I check in to see if I'm still aligned with my Soul or if I've strayed off course.

As I sit and contemplate this, uncovering and discovering ideas, blocks, thoughts, prayers, and wishes, I listen to the earth energy around me. I ask the sun held high in the sky, the rose bursting from her bud, the rocks guiding the fresh water what they think. The answer is always the same: "*You* are the purpose."

It's simple, really. And yet as humans, we've overcomplicated purpose to be a way of working too hard, earning loads of money, and impressing our peers. We work to numb our pain, prove our worth, and outdo each other. While devotion to work and an income are both necessary elements of purpose, it's also important to have fun, listen to the cycles within, and live in the fullness of our truth.

My truth may unfold as a new book or oracle set, or as a day in the garden planting seeds. It may be a conversation with a mentor that I'm needing, or a few hours on the couch writing poetry. It may be a refresh of my website or social media, or a local adventure with my kids. If it's a directive of my heart, *it's all purpose.*

Your purpose isn't only your work, it's your whole life. To live on purpose, you must be true to who you are and what you need and desire in every moment. It's simply honoring yourself right now for your power, gifts, talents, and love.

Selfish is only thinking of yourself, *selfless* is only thinking of others, *Oneness* is living as though both are important and the same.

Live in Oneness with all of life and allow *the grand and wild purpose* of your Soul to unfold like a flower in divine and aligned timing.

• RITUAL •
Listening Presence Conversations

I've found that the most important offering you can share with someone in need is a compassionate, open-minded, kind-hearted, listening practice.

The next time you find yourself in a conversation with someone who is having a difficult time, try as often as you can to be quiet and listen. Here are a few ways to sink into deep listening:

- Let there be spacious pauses. The more you listen, the more they will share, and the deeper their healing will be. Don't fill the gaps with your story; just allow for the space to be.

- Let them cry and be upset without saying, "It's okay." Let them speak and share from their heart without unnecessary interruption.

- The magic is your presence. When your presence is consciously spacious and palpably loving, there's room for the other to soften and let go. Holding space for another happens when we trust that sometimes there's nothing to do, no one we need to be, other than the energy of love. Love heals all.

We all need each other for this reason. Some conversations will be like a dance, both partners sharing equally, vivaciously, loudly. Other conversations call for us to be open to our ancient presence, for which no words can ever substitute.

LOVE IS ALL THERE IS

In the great heights and dark depths of your life's journey, you'll find love. Love is always there holding you close, guiding you onward, accepting you fully, and seeing you in all your magic. As we complete this journey in the wild, I pray you feel the love that lives within you in every moment.

· JOURNEY ·
Love All the Way Home

On the home stretch of this passage, you've fallen in love with your wild self so many times and in countless ways that now there's no time when you're not in love. Life is one long, loving communion with your friends, the earth, your beloved, and your spirit.

Your beloved comes and goes, their loving presence ever near no matter where their physical form resides. You've made promises to take care of each other for as long as you're joyfully wound together while you also honor your independent adventures and solitary restoration.

You're so enraptured with the spacious present moment that you loosen your attachment to what used to be important.

You're so in love with life that you've forgotten your fear of death, and you humbly sit with those whose spirits are passing to the higher places.

This love, this nurturing energy that swirls and spills all over and through you, is the highest purpose you've reached on your inner journey. Love is all you need, for it calls you to your purpose though serving, it opens you to giving and receiving, it holds you in the darkest nights, and it carries to you all forms of abundance and health.

With two hands on your heart and your eyes to the sky, you recognize with deep humility and absolute rapture that you've achieved your heart's greatest goal on this wildhearted journey ... *to be love*.

THE ANSWER IS LOVE

When you know deep, deep down that your loving presence here on this enchanted earth is purpose enough, you'll leave behind the striving, fear, hustle, and excess and focus on what you can do to be a whole and loving being each day.

By expanding, not pushing. By embracing, not denying. By anticipating, not expecting. By deciding, not controlling. By allowing, not resisting.

And if you're ever in doubt about what that means or how to find your truth, if you're ever concerned that you're not doing enough or finding your way, tune in to your heart. Your heart is a portal to the whole Universe. Your heart has the answer, *and the answer is love.*

Love is who you are and why you're here. Love created you and walks with you. Love lives all the way within and around you.

Love is the purpose and *the purpose is love.*

CONCLUSION
AND GRATITUDE

I'm so grateful you created space in your life to adventure through this book with me. I hope these words landed softly among the sweet folds of your heart and also ignited a powerful urge within the unending trails of your being to live free, untethered, and illuminated on your unmapped path.

You are a creature of nature, molded by the earth, awakened by stars, and tuned in to the cycles of the Universe. May you always, *always* trust your infinite heart and ancient Soul. May you dream, play, and live as though *everything* is possible.

You, divine reader, are the reason I am living my sweet purpose. Thank you for opening your heart and this book.

As our wildhearted journey together comes to an end, may this be the beginning of your own beautiful, infinite, and abundant journey into the wilderness of your Soul.

Should you ever feel lost as you venture through the dark on unpaved paths, know that Love has your hand and knows intimately the blueprint of your Soul. Trust in Love. It will take you home.

Blessings and love,

Kris

Acknowledgments

Mother Earth, thank you for your inspiration and abundance. I am full of gratitude for everything you provide me with in this life and that you chose me to write this book for you. May every word honor you and speak of your profound lifeforce and plentiful love.

Mom and Dad, thank you for taking me to the outback, the beach, and the snow; into caves, over mountains, and onto islands. Thank you for following your hearts across the earth and back and taking us with you. And thank you for honoring my wild ways.

Mark, thank you for being the sovereign, strong tree to my impulsive, whimsical wildflower. I love you and your steady ways. I'm so grateful to call you my beloved...and live in the luscious rainforest with you.

Lucas, thank you for making me a mama. You have your dad's unshakableness, which I appreciate and revere. You are such a kind, funny, and wholehearted boy. I love you.

Ariella, thank you for choosing me to be your mama. You mirror my wild beauty, you teach me about presence, and you align me with the pulse of Her. I love you.

Antara Rose, I hold you in the stars, sister, and I love you and your wildly generous heart.

Sarah McLeod, goddess of prayer and infinite healing, thank you for walking beside me during the weaving of this message. I love you and how much you care for humanity.

Tash and Dylan, I'm so grateful to walk, eat, garden, play, and laugh beside you both and your beautiful, wild baby. Thank you for reminding me of the power of nature, and for trusting me on that Thursday morning in early fall. I love you sweet family.

Miranda Short, thank you for showing me your secret, sacred beach spot where the seed for this book was planted. Gratitude to you beautiful woman for reminding me of the importance of skinny-dipping my way through life. I love you.

Rachel Pascoe, your infinite encouragement all throughout the writing and editing of this book and beyond has made the process ever more joyful. I love you and the wild you reflect in me.

Love and gratitude to everyone in my community; you all inspire and uplift me in more ways than I can ever explain. You are a resilient, loving, incredible bunch of goddesses and warriors who show me how to live my truth every day.

To all the incredibly talented collaborators at Llewellyn, your gifts make the expression of my words that much more tangible, beautiful, and articulate. Angela Wix, thank you for holding this vision with me from the very first moment. Your heartfelt editing support is cherished so deeply. Cassie Willett, your exquisite cover is beyond my wild heart's dreams, thank you. Mandie Brasington, so much gratitude for your attention to detail curating the inner design of this book. Sami Sherratt, your endless patience and editing gifts are appreciated beyond words.

And you, wild and glorious reader, this was all for you.

Bibliography

Aletta, Lauren. *Into the Woods.* Queensland, Australia: Inner Hue, 2017.

Brand, Russell. *Revolution.* London: Arrow, 2015.

Brown, Brené. *Atlas of the Heart: Mapping Meaningful Connection and the Language of Human Experience.* London: Vermilion, 2021.

———. *Daring Greatly: How the Courage to Be Vulnerable Transforms the Way We Live, Love, Parent, and Lead.* New York: Avery, 2012.

Cameron, Julia. *The Artist's Way: A Spiritual Path to Higher Creativity.* New York: J. P. Tarcher/Putnam, 1992.

Doyle, Glennon. *Untamed.* New York: The Dial Press, 2020.

Elenna, Elen. *Silver Wheel: The Lost Teachings of the Deerskin Book.* London: Head of Zeus, 2016.

Gilbert, Elizabeth. *Big Magic: Creative Living Beyond Fear.* New York: Bloomsbury Publishing, 2015.

Hand Clow, Barbara. *Alchemy of Nine Dimensions: The 2011/2012 Prophecies and Nine Dimensions of Consciousness.* Charlottesville, VA: Hampton Roads Publishing, 2010.

Hawkins, David R. *Letting Go: The Pathway of Surrender.* Carlsbad, CA: Hay House, 2012.

Jagat, Guru. *Invincible Living: The Power of Yoga, the Energy of Breath, and Other Tools for a Radiant Life.* San Francisco, CA: HarperCollins, 2017.

LaPorte, Danielle. *White Hot Truth: Clarity for Keeping it Real on Your Spiritual Path from One Seeker to Another.* Vancouver: Virtuonica, 2017.

McLeod, Sarah. *Spirit Guidance: Vision Weaving with Healing Energy.* Schenectady, NY: Citrine, 2020.

Murphy-Hiscock, Arin. *The Green Witch: Your Complete Guide to the Natural Magic of Herbs, Flowers, Essentials Oils, and More.* Avon, MA: Adams Media, 2017.

Myss, Caroline. *Anatomy of the Spirit: The Seven Stages of Power and Healing.* Great Britain: Bantam Books, 1997.

Osho. *Creativity: Unleashing the Forces Within.* New York: Griffin, 1999.

Rasha. *Oneness.* Sante Fe, NM: Earthstar, 2003.

Silver, Tosha. *Outrageous Openness: Letting the Divine Take the Lead.* New York: Simon & Schuster, 2014.

Starr, Mirabai. *Wild Mercy: Living the Fierce and Tender Wisdom of the Women Mystics.* Boulder, CO: Sounds True, 2019.

Tolle, Eckhart. *A New Earth: Awakening to Your Life's Purpose.* New York: Penguin, 2005.

Walsch, Neale Donald. *Conversations with God: An Uncommon Dialogue, Book 2.* London: Hodder and Stoughton, 1997.

Watkins, Alfred. *The Old Straight Track: Its Mounds, Beacons, Moats, Sites and Mark Stones.* Heritage Hunter, 2015.

STAY CONNECTED

I'd love to support you on your wildhearted journey.

Soul Sessions. To work with me personally and find spirited insight on your wildhearted purpose: www.krisfranken.com /sessions.

Heartfelt Meditations. For access to meditations that calm, inspire, uplift, and bring you closer to your heart: www.krisfranken .com/meditations.

Conscious Healing Retreats. Join me on healing retreats: www .krisfranken.com/retreats.

To buy a copy of my book *The Call of Intuition*: www.krisfranken .com/thecallofintuition.

Connect on Instagram and Pinterest: @kris_franken.

TO WRITE TO THE AUTHOR

If you wish to contact the author or would like more information about this book, please write to the author in care of Llewellyn Worldwide Ltd. and we will forward your request. Both the author and the publisher appreciate hearing from you and learning of your enjoyment of this book and how it has helped you. Llewellyn Worldwide Ltd. cannot guarantee that every letter written to the author can be answered, but all will be forwarded. Please write to:

Kris Franken
℅ Llewellyn Worldwide
2143 Wooddale Drive
Woodbury, MN 55125-2989

Please enclose a self-addressed stamped envelope for reply,
or $1.00 to cover costs. If outside the U.S.A., enclose
an international postal reply coupon.

Many of Llewellyn's authors have websites with additional
information and resources. For more information,
please visit our website at http://www.llewellyn.com.